Building a Movement to End
the New Jim Crow

an organizing guide

The Veterans of Hope Project

Building a Movement to End the New Jim Crow: an organizing guide
ISBN #978-0-9885508-1-0, Published by the Veterans of Hope Project
© 2015 Daniel Hunter. All rights reserved.

The Veterans of Hope Project is a multifaceted educational initiative on religion, culture, and participatory democracy. We encourage a healing-centered approach to community-building that recognizes the interconnectedness of spirit, creativity, and citizenship. Our educational materials are designed to support reconciliation, nonviolence, and an appreciation for the value of indigenous and folk wisdom for contemporary times.

This booklet emerged from conversations among Daniel Hunter, Daryl Atkinson, Chris Moore-Backman, Michelle Alexander, and the late Dr. Vincent Harding. It was inspired by *The New Jim Crow Study Guide and Call to Action* (Denver, CO: Veterans of Hope 2013), available at www.NewJimCrowOrganizing.org.

Cover image used with permission, from the paperback edition of Michelle Alexander's *The New Jim Crow* (New York: The New Press, 2010, 2012). For more information about Michelle Alexander, www.NewJimCrow.com. For more information about The New Press, www.TheNewPress.com.

Back cover photo by Shadia Fayne Wood, www.projectsurvivalmedia.org. Drawings inside the book are by Joshua Kahn Russell, joshuakahnrussell.wordpress.com. Design of front cover created by author with help from Kaytee Riek, www.kayteeriek.com.

Dedicated to the life and teachings of Dr. Vincent Harding, a friend and confidant of Rev. Martin Luther King Jr., who eldered generations of activists.

In the words of Maya Angelou:

And when great souls die,
after a period peace blooms,
slowly and always
irregularly. Spaces fill
with a kind of
soothing electric vibration.
Our senses, restored, never
to be the same, whisper to us.
They existed. They existed.
We can be. Be and be
better. For they existed.

To the memory of him and all the other teachers, elders, poets, prophets, and griots who have come before us.

ACKNOWLEDGMENTS

There are so many people in this struggle. All of them deserve more acknowledgment and praise for their commitment, efforts, and dedication. In that spirit, I thank everyone who is teaching us how to strive for justice, both those who let me use their stories in this book and those whose stories I didn't have the space to tell.

I'm grateful to those who gave feedback and advice on drafts: Michelle Alexander, Clarissa Rogers, Hilary Beard, Dr. Phyllis Boanes, Pamela Haines, Nico Amador, Bhavana Nancherla, Lori Kenshaft, Eileen Flannegan, Bob and Carol Hunter, Lunden Abelson, and Judy Meikle. Thanks to my most excellent copy editor, Suzy Subways, and to Ryan Lietner for outreach. Thanks to everyone who helped with design, including designer Kaytee Riek, artist Joshua Kahn Russell, and photographer Shadia Fayne Wood; and for image permissions, The New Press. Thanks to Rebecca Subar's West Chester class for research: Jess Gregan, Katie Lyons, Kyle Phillips, Sarah Stamm, Brianna Swartz, Julius Taliaferro, Mallory Spencer, Bruce Yockey, Courtney Mowen, and Julian Goss.

Thanks to Chris Moore-Backman for your eternal patience—this never would have happened without you. And also to my advisors on this project: the insightful Daryl Atkinson and the incomparable late Dr. Vincent Harding.

Finally, thanks to everyone who supported this project via crowdsourcing:

M Abare, N Almassi, F Anderson, J Anderson, A Anemone, V Anthony, Anonymous, B Apostol, J Arceneaux, M Armstead, G Atwood, J Bacon, S Barnett, D Barry, T Baskin, E Basom, H Beard, A Berry, T Blake, H Box, N Boyce, J Bradley, M Bradshaw, M O'Brien, J Broach, S Brody, G Browne, J Butler, A Carchedi, J Carroll, M Carter, Central Baptist Wayne, R Cecil, M Charest, S Chase, B Clare, J Cocks, J CordonHill, S Crossley, M Cristina Cuerda, J Culley, J Cummings, A Cytron-Walker, R Dance, N Daniel, L Davis, R Davis, K DeJong, N Devani, A William Diebolt, L Dodge, D Donovan, J Dowell, L Duncan, S Dunham, A Dunn, E DuVerlie, W Elling, A Erde, N Fior, C Fisher-Borne, E Flanagan, J Frank, R Frost, C Furman, M Fusoni, M Gagne, M Galvis, M Garmo, A Gehres, J Gelbspan, J Gingold, S Gish-Kraus, J Glaspie, C Blythe & R Goodman, L Gould, J Gowen, L Gray, S Joy Green, J Carl Gregg, S Griss, A Lisa Gross, R Hadley, P Haines, H Hammond, D Hartsough, M Hawthorn, Haymarket People's Fund, L Held, N Helfrich, I Hempseed, B Beckel & J Hesla, A Hill, C Hodelin, A Hoffman, P Holden, C Horwitz, D Hostetler, B Huebner, B & C Hunter, F Imberman, J Isard, P Ives, L Jackson, P James, R Janis, Jeanne-Marie, L Margot Johnson, L Johnson, M Johnson, T Johnson, P Jones, T Rashima Jordan, K Kamisugi, R Kean, A Kelly, L Kenschaft, B Kieft, A Kietzman, C Klug, E Koopman, C Kutz, S LaChappelle, I Lakey, landskov, A Lang, J Langdon, J Lapham, J Lashof, R LaVallee, M Lechner, G Leever, G Leondar-Wright, J Lewis, T Lindley, W Lofton, N Long, G Lopez, S Taylor & A Loving, R Luban, S Macbride, C MacDonald-Dennis, S Madeira, madeleih, V Madrigal, A Mahvash, H Malcomson, T Mammel, L Manders, Y Marom, J McDonough, J Mcleod, mdolliole, J Meikle, K Meister, A Mercurio, G Metzger, michfarq8212, E Miller, D Montgomery, R Moran, N Morice, M Muhammad, R Muhammad, J Murrian, K O'Neill, C Nelson, P Nelson, K Nero, B Nestor, K Neuringer, G Newbold, J Newton, J Nikelsky, B O'Connor, C Odelugo, D Olasky, S Olshevski, X Ortiz-Gonzalez, N Ostrand, M Overton, L Padilla, H Page, K Palmer, A Parra, M Pate, F Paynter, T Pease, P Pedemonti, C Peterson, T Peterson, A Pettus, K Parr Philipson, V Pigatt, M Pillischer, L Polaski, L Powell-Haney, D Preiser, J Priest, S Pritikin, rabbilynn, D Radin, R Revelle, J Rewa, rewel0013, K Ridd, M Ray & K Riek, R Rifkin, B Riley, J Riley, M Riley, C Robinson, D Banks Robinson, D Rooney, M Rozycki, rpneyman, A Ruga, E Sabel, E Sanders, M Sanderson, R Sandow, sandrar.hart, B Savage, P Scenck, S Schmidt, D Schroeder, K Schwab, S Schweik, S Sheridan, R Short, T Siftar, D Simmons, C Simpson, sincecombahee, F Skellie III, J Skinner, R Slajda, D Smith, E Smith, S Smith, B Solow, L Solyntjes, N Spann, B Spiers, C Springer-Lockhart, sschmidt, M Stafford, M Stein, S Stengel, C Stewart, K Stokes, K Sue, T & W Hjelt Sullivan, D Suzuki-Brobeck, N Szwergold, t4k.core, M Tahaie, G Tarver Jr, D & P Taylor, P Taylor, theajohnson, M Thompson, S James Thompson II, T Thompson, E Thorne, D Tilsen, A Trost, B Turner, A Varma, N Maxwell Vassilakis, E Vesely-Flad, A W, L Wagner, J Walker, M Walker, S Walton, S Welna, B West, K Wheeler, S Wiggins, B Willeford, C Williams, K Wilson, and N Wolfe & S Zunes.

CONTENTS

FOREWORD

There is more activism in the United States today than we have seen since the Black Freedom and Justice campaigns that so deeply impacted our nation during the tumultuous twenty-year span of 1953 to 1973. US activism today expresses frustration and even rage over a broad spectrum of oppressive systems that abuse an enormous number of people. Most of these systems are intimately related to one another, though their convergence is not well understood or identified in public discourse.

The unsettling truth, however, is that too much of the activism today is for the sake of activism and does not move public awareness or public action in the needed direction. It is my contention that if activism is to move our nation toward a genuine experience of equality, justice, and the beloved community, we must deliberately employ the unimaginable power of nonviolent civil resistance. This is soul force (*satyagraha*), a term invented by Mohandas Gandhi that pulls together his experiments in bold, creative, and carefully planned actions that can dismantle unjust systems and provide breathing room for new, life-affirming possibilities.

This booklet, *Building a Movement to End the New Jim Crow*, seeks to focus people in the direction of dismantling our nation's huge and egregious prison industrial systems, the old but new Jim Crow. In it, Daniel Hunter describes key organizing principles and offers an array of examples that describe concrete ways that individuals, organizations, and coalitions are achieving significant successes, which cultivate the soil for more and more significant campaigns in this crucial struggle.

I like what the people described in these pages are doing! They have discovered their community of struggle, and they have identified the changes they seek. They show forth ways of being and working together in kinship and with coherence. They demonstrate personal transformation exerting life and engendering power. They act in unity around the projects they have adopted. In short, they reflect Gandhi's approach to nonviolent resistance and struggle, the "force more powerful" that the movement to end mass incarceration, and US activism in general, so desperately need.

Rev. James Lawson, February 2015, Los Angeles

INTRODUCTION

A group of folks who read *The New Jim Crow* asked me for advice. They agreed with Michelle Alexander's contention that mass incarceration is an appalling system echoing the racist social dynamics that created slavery and Jim Crow. Inspired by the book, they organized monthly speakers and events. They did their best to educate others about the far-reaching impacts of the system and its basis of labeling people as "other" to oppress them.

They felt good about the educational work they were doing—but also felt like they were tilling the soil without planting seeds in the ground. They sensed they could be doing more and asked: "What can we do to make a bigger impact?"

They wanted to make a difference. However, they were spending more time studying the dynamics of the problems than the dynamics of making change. As a result, they fell prey to the belief that social change is just education and personal expression and didn't understand how to fully exercise their power to catalyze transformation.

In the midst of India's struggle for freedom from British Rule, Mohandas Gandhi said to his people: "It is not a matter of carrying conviction by argument. The matter resolves itself into one of matching forces. Conviction or no conviction, Great Britain would defend her Indian commerce and interests by all the forces at her command. India must consequently evolve force enough to free herself from that embrace of death."[1]

Those who most benefit from the current prison system will defend it. We therefore need to learn to wage struggle for a new society unwilling to allow any human life to be thought of as expendable, that doesn't mask problems by throwing people behind bars.

This booklet is for members of that group and others like them, who want to move into social action. It does not offer a secret recipe for foolproof organizing. No such recipe exists (and beware of anyone who tries to convince you otherwise!). It does offer concrete, tested tools and activities you can use in groups. It's filled with practical tips and strategic principles, with real-life examples from this and other movements. At the end of each section are guiding questions to help you and your group think about next steps.

Chapter 1 looks at the *different roles played in movements*, with an encouragement for each of us to recognize our own strengths while appreciating those of others. This is especially important with such a wide-ranging movement, where people are working on everything from halting police harassment, stopping new prisons, changing laws on disproportionate sentencing, ending solitary confinement, eliminating job and housing discrimination, increasing funding for reentry programs, and providing medical care for all to rebuilding our shattered schools and ending the growing school-to-prison pipeline.

Chapter 2 looks at *building strong groups*. Groups help us connect our story with the stories of others. Groups build communal strength to act outside of apathy, shame, or lofty unapplied ideals. Groups generate social power and are a building block of movement work.

Chapter 3 looks at creating change through *campaigns*. Campaigns harness the power of groups and direct that power toward a single goal. With intention and focus, campaigns create pressure to enact specific, concrete changes. By making these changes, we can chip away at the larger oppressive system and hone our ability to transform society.

My hope is that the organizing principles, tools, and stories presented in this booklet will help those who read it play an active role in building a movement powerful enough to end the New Jim Crow—a movement to not merely reform the current system, but one that will bring about deep-rooted and lasting structural change.

CHAPTER 1
ROLES IN MOVEMENT-BUILDING

P elican Bay State Prison has been deemed one of the ten worst prisons in the United States, and its Security Housing Unit (SHU) one of the most notorious.[2] The 1,200 people locked in the SHU are placed in 7 x 11 foot cells, locked inside for at least 22 hours a day, and fed through a slot in the cell door to limit any semblance of human contact. It was there that a group of people organized hunger strikes, unaware that their actions would create waves around the country.

The SHU was allegedly formed as an attempt to break up gang activity. In one wing, jailers put four men, each a suspected gang leader, in separate cells: Todd Ashker, Sitawa Jamaa, Arturo Castellanos, and Antonio Guillen—supposedly of the Aryan Brotherhood, Black Guerrilla Family, Mexican Mafia, and Nuestra Familia, respectively.

The four were locked in their own cells, unable to see anyone or a shred of natural light. Still, over the course of years, they talked to each other, shouting through narrow slats or toilet drains. They built relationship and connection, their rival gang status notwithstanding. After prolonged discussion, in 2011 they decided to launch the first of what would turn out to be many hunger strikes.

The initial strike was a drop in the bucket compared to what would come later.[3] It won only minor concessions: a small handball and a single pull-up bar in the otherwise bare exercise room. And the action was largely ignored by the mainstream media—who failed to detect the movement underway.

However, the strike inspired a wave of other hunger strikers. Hearing about the actions through various networks, people in prisons across Ohio, North Carolina, Illinois, Virginia, and other states followed suit and organized their own strikes. Almost 6,500 incarcerated people participated in this first strike.

In 2013, the Pelican Bay SHU struck again. This coordinated hunger strike was larger and extended 59-days. At its peak, it included nearly 30,000 incarcerated people across California prisons—and many more across the country and globe. Suddenly the issue of solitary confinement was on the national agenda, with media reporting as if they had known about the issue for years.[4]

That sense of momentum and growing energy is what marks a *movement*. Like the black freedom movement, the abolitionist movement against slavery, or the farmworkers movement, *movements* are forces of collective energy, channeling deep emotions like anger and love and mobilized by hopes and dreams for large-scale change.

There is great power in movements. Unfortunately, popular culture and history do us a major disservice in how they present social change movements (if they present them at all). They teach myths that have to be unlearned if we are to build an effective movement against mass incarceration.

Myth: Movements are lit like a match.

In reality, the original 2011 hunger strike took five years to build. The four men needed to build trust, talking about their personal lives and settling on a strategy. Yet a history textbook might skip all of that and begin the story with tens of thousands of people in the larger strikes of 2013. The myth that movements "suddenly appear" misses the critical process of building up networks ready to act and ways to communicate broadly. The myth ignores the necessary tasks of leadership building and visioning. While sparks are important, without these critical pieces, movements will not turn into a fire.

Myth: Movements are built by heroic figurehead leaders.

While we may think of Martin Luther King Jr., or Mohandas Gandhi, or Cesar Chavez, or even those four initial hunger strikers at

Pelican Bay as the heroic leaders, movements are far more dynamic than that. They are built by many organizations, groups, and loose-knit networks that organize and act together for change.

Myth: Movements require complete internal unity.

We can look with rose-colored glasses on the past, making it appear as though movements were unified, often under the direction of a charismatic leader. Each hunger strike was a blow against injustice, but they didn't have the exact same goals or approaches. Successful movements always have internal disagreements and division. Working for unity is great, but so is accepting the reality that ideological purity isn't a requirement for us to engage and continue in a movement together.

Myth: Movements succeed if they mobilize large, mass actions.

Countless times the refrain is made: "We just need to have a giant March on Washington." However, movements don't win because of singular actions. Movements need ongoing resistance—otherwise, the powerholders can just wait until the march is over and continue ignoring movement requests. Movements require sustained pressure for change at many levels. It takes time to build, but without ongoing resistance, movements don't achieve their goals.

Each of these myths that we are taught makes us look externally, whether for the heroic leader, the right circumstances, or the big mass action. But movements are most effective when we look inward and find strength in ourselves and our relationships. To do this, one starting point is understanding the different roles people play in movements, so we can find our own best way to participate and contribute.

UNDERSTAND YOUR ROLE IN SOCIAL CHANGE

To reach its goal, a movement must include different approaches to change and a great variety of people filling different roles. Each of us prefer some roles over others. And we may play a range of different roles in different circumstances. Understanding our preferences and strengths can help us work with others more powerfully. A civil rights activist came up with a useful framework that describes different social change roles: *Helpers, Advocates, Organizers,* and *Rebels.*[5] There may be many other roles in social change, but it's a helpful start to compare and contrast some roles that frequently show up in movements.

Helpers are people who see an individual in need and try to meet that need. Helpers often provide direct service, such as opening their homes, educating about job interviews, offering therapy for family members, or feeding hungry people. They open their hearts and respond personally with the resources they have available.

Advocates see a need but also see systems out there with resources, even if they're broken and unfair. Advocates help people navigate those systems, perhaps doing social work, public advocacy, or impact litigation. They use knowledge of the system to help people fill their needs, bending the system so it provides every ounce of justice or resources it can provide.

Organizers have another approach. When looking at problems, their instinct is to bring together those who are hurting. They often organize people outside the system into groups to apply pressure to change the rules of the system. Unlike Helpers, who provide direct services, or Advocates, who tend to work inside the system, Organizers traditionally create pressure by building groups external to the current system.

Rebels, driven by passion and energy, speak truth to power and do so with conviction. They are associated with public protest and direct action, using tactics like sit-ins, marches, and civil disobedience. Rebels are impatient with small reforms and are uncompromising in their struggle for major changes in society. Rebels are often public in their work, even if it might carry personal risk for them.

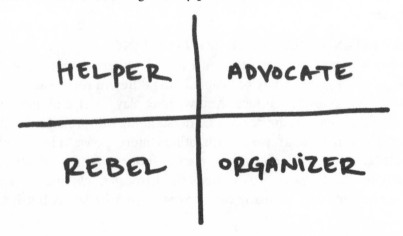

Each role is important. Yet you probably have your own preferences about which roles most attract you. Knowing your own preferences can help you fulfill your role more effectively—and work with others who are in equally important, but different, roles. Let's look a little more closely at these four different roles in social change, including examples of their work and their different strengths and potential weaknesses.

HELPERS

Helpers offer shelter, food, and caring to those in need. In the process, they make face-to-face and heart-to-heart connections with people. They try to offer services to help every single person they can. Helpers are immensely important to those getting services, and it can be very rewarding for them, too.

Helpers can also do things that are less effective. If Helpers are unconscious of the need for structural change, their work may be solely about feel-good band-aids. Helpers may treat it like a personal failing that someone out of prison cannot find a job—not recognizing structural components, such as the infamous "box" that requires job applicants to divulge their criminal history. Helpers can therefore create cycles of dependency.

To be effective, Helpers must also support people to see how the system places stumbling blocks in their lives. This helps people rise above individual self-sabotage and self-recrimination, potentially clearing the way for them to participate in movement work.

Take the Albert Cobarrubias Justice Project (ACJP).[6] They got their start doing the work of Helpers in a drop-in center. People working assembly jobs in Silicon Valley—the low-wage underside of the "tech bubble"—would get help and support. Over time they became known for helping people beat false criminal charges and providing support through the justice system. A tally showed their efforts, through acquittals or reduced sentences, saved people over 1,800 years in prison!

Yet ACJP strives to do more than just serve individuals. Take Gail Noble, whose son was swept up by police and charged with assault and battery, despite witnesses saying he wasn't involved. Her son's attorney was ill-prepared and shrugged off a "joke" made by the judge that her son's summer job was probably just a cover for "going door to door selling drugs."

At a Sunday meeting of the ACJP, Gail shared her story. Folks at ACJP listened and offered to help her file a motion to fire her son's attorney. "Even though the judge refused my son's motion," says Gail, "it was important to get all the issues my son had [with the lawyer] on record and for us to feel that we could speak and say something."[7]

ACJP's work with Gail could have ended when her son was sentenced to eight months. Instead they helped her write her story for their magazine and chose the case as a front page story. They asked her to join the Sunday meetings to help others with their cases. She began to work with ACJP to influence the selection process for the next police chief. And when the state tried to pass "tough on crime" legislation, she headed the march into the district attorney's office.

Far from a one-way service relationship, the approach of ACJP brought directly impacted people together. ACJP used the trust built by directly helping to move beyond individual struggles and into larger structural issues to create even bigger ripples of change.

ADVOCATES

Advocates, such as lawyers or social workers, help individuals survive and navigate the rules and regulations of the current system. With their inside knowledge of policies and protocols, visionary advocates can offer meaningful changes to the current system or even comprehensive alternatives.

As with Helpers, Advocates can have their blinders. Their years studying the ins and outs of the courts or the public benefits system can get in the way. Unintentionally, Advocates can dampen people's desire for radical change by urging that they accept the system as it is: "You can't do that, because there's a regulation against it!" Instead of using their expertise to creatively and vigorously fight for long-term change, some Advocates can be guilty of focusing on all the barriers in the current system to new ways of working and thinking.

Eager to help, Advocates can get stuck in an attitude that they should be able to solve all their clients' problems, without promoting their clients' agency or vision. The client relationship becomes one-directional: helping is something that happens to you, so you aren't part of your own liberation.

But it doesn't have to be that way. Daryl Atkinson, a member of the Formerly Incarcerated and Convicted People's Movement and a criminal justice lawyer with Southern Coalition for Social Justice, got his start through the mentorship of a transformational Advocate, James McConico.[8] Daryl and James met while both were locked up in a maximum security facility. "James was a jailhouse lawyer with a law collective on the inside," said Daryl. "He was real good. When the yard call went out, there was a long wait for him. He would do a lot of work for people inside—but he did it conditionally."[9]

Daryl describes one day when he and James were with a young man from the Crips gang. The young man sat across from James with a pillowcase full of cigarettes and offered the pillowcase as payment for legal advice.

James shook his head. "I don't smoke. If you want my help, you have to drop your colors in the cell block. And you have to learn the Bill of Rights and you have to join us in this fight." The young man was startled by the unusual request. James wasn't selling advice, he was using legal services to change men's lives. He was building a group of people to change their lives inside and outside of prison. Beyond filing writs in their cases, he was helping people find agency, hope, and purpose. The young man agreed to the requests.

People like Daryl now carry on that style of transformational advocacy, which creates a powerful ripple effect and grows the movement.

ORGANIZERS

Organizers often critique Helpers and Advocates for helping a broken system limp along—rather than abolishing or changing the system. The classic Organizer story is that of a village near a river. Each day the villagers find an abandoned baby floating down the river, and each day the villagers take the baby in and care for it. After several weeks, one of the villagers gets fed up at the cycle. She walks around the village convincing everyone the problem will never stop unless they walk up the river and find out where all the babies are coming from! That approach is fundamental to good Organizers:

identifying root causes and bringing people together to solve problems, with a belief that they can build power to make change.

Organizers, however, can be ineffective when they get bogged down in the inner life of their groups. They might get stuck in a stifling nonprofit or in the belief that they should only go after goals *they* deem "winnable"—even when the people most affected are urging otherwise. Organizers who are not directly impacted, especially, may fall into assuming leadership roles rather than empowering the people most impacted to take on leadership for themselves.

By contrast, take Steve Huerta, a formerly incarcerated activist and organizer in San Antonio, Texas. After conducting an electoral power analysis in his area, Steve learned that in Bexar County, the Democratic Party was relying on votes from incarcerated people and their families. Research showed that almost 75% of the precinct chairs were formerly incarcerated, had misdemeanors, or had family members in prison. But when it came time to make policy, they consistently ran from their people and favored "tough on crime" legislation. To solve the problem, Steve decided to out-organize the traditional party by building a group of formerly incarcerated people who had worked against such "tough on crime" legislation and having them run for local Democratic seats.

Steve believed the shame of being incarcerated or even being related to "convicts" kept people from standing up for what is right. Organizers understand that shame festers and breeds when people experience something as a personal failing they cannot overcome. He challenged that shame by getting people together and showing how their background made them experts on what needed to change. In the words of a judge he worked with, "The system likes to make your mistakes count against you. But you flip it. You make it not a list of a record of past mistakes, but a resume of how you're an expert on a policy that exists."

Steve uses that resume to build up a group of people with classic community-based organizing. "My approach is basically door-to-door and face-to-face," he explains. "We hang out at grocery stores. ATMs. Food Stamp offices. Wherever people get things they need. And we explain to them who we are. When we first explain we are former prisoners, that gets their attention. Then when we tell them we are recruiting them to be active in challenging the Democratic Party—they *really* take notice."

Through this approach, Steve and his coworkers have helped formerly incarcerated people get elected as local precinct chairs. In 2014, Steve was elected as a senate district committeeperson representing about half a million people. Having people who are bought-in to policy changes on mass incarceration has made a major shift in the Democratic conventions. "We're getting people to show up to these conventions," Steve explains, "And they see people they respect being engaged and having a voice. It's very empowering."

Those wins come because he's modeling what good organizers do: gathering people together, creating space for people to tell their stories, and putting them in the leadership of the movement. With his face-to-face style and "we'll-out-organize-you" know-how, he's putting formerly incarcerated people with a change agenda directly into power positions—both inside his group and in positions of official policy decision-making.

REBELS

Lastly, there are the *Rebels*. Rebels bring fire and energy and are willing to take risks that others may never even consider. They can be unyielding in pursuit of justice and willing to go through great personal sacrifice to make their point. Many political prisoners, for example, are Rebels who came out of political and social movements and have gone on to teach people that deep change is needed and it often takes sacrifice to make it happen.

However, Rebels can become ineffective when they are too attached to a marginal identity, use tactics without a realistic strategy, or self-righteously view everyone else as less radical or less moral. Rebels can be guilty of too often tearing down ideas and saying "No!" rather then being constructive. They do their best work when they are well connected to people in other roles who can give context to Rebels' unique, bold, and essential contributions.

As an example, after one organization's high-profile lobbying efforts had fallen short, they brought in a trainer to teach them how to run a direct action campaign. The trainer described the four roles of social change and asked people to cluster with others in the same roles. They had a handful of Helpers, many Advocates, and a good number of Organizers—but no Rebels. When asked about this, the group admitted that there used to be Rebels, but they were hard to work with and over time had been encouraged to leave. The trainer promptly announced that they could end the workshop now, explaining, "Without Rebels, you can't run a direct action campaign."

Rebels point fingers at problems that may go unnoticed, and they can be decisively bold about it. At a national gathering of correctional personnel, a group called Sisters Inside decided to dramatize the harassment of women in prisons. They seized the stage and acted out a strip search, with some people playing prisoners and others the guards. Telling the story, Angela Davis writes, "The gathering was so repulsed by this enactment of a practice that occurs routinely in women's prisons everywhere that many of the participants felt compelled to disassociate themselves from such practices.... Some of the guards...simply cried upon watching representations of their own actions outside the prison context."[10] Rebels' boldness can shock, awaken, and help stoke anger for change.

RESPECT THE MANY ROLES FOR CHANGE

Each role is vital in movement-building: Helpers' direct services, Advocates' accessing resources inside the system, Organizers' pulling people together to struggle for their own solutions, and Rebels' in-your-face actions that speak truth to power. Again, these four are not the only roles—but they are a sampling of different roles played in social change.

Each role has its own approach to change—and that's important, because movements need these varied approaches. Yet these approaches can be a source of tension. Organizers often get frustrated by Helpers who don't connect their service work to larger issues. Or Rebels can get angry at Advocates who don't dream outside the current system. Advocates may be frustrated with Organizers who don't value the real ways their advocacy helps make change. Or Helpers can feel discounted by Rebels and feel the Rebels' pounding insistence turns people off.

Yet movements are best when all the roles are appreciated, recognized, and filled. Our job is to contribute our particular gifts to the movement, knowing that all are important and trusting that others will fill in the spaces we're not called to fill.

Jerry Elster's journey exemplifies how many different roles can make positive impacts toward movement-building. His story starts in the rough streets of South Central Los Angeles. After spending some time in a juvenile camp for petty vandalism, Jerry tried to get his life on the right track, deciding "I was above the gang stuff, I was through with that foolishness."[11] To send himself through college, he tried a variety of odd jobs. None were steady. He resorted to selling weed.

From there he slipped into gang life and all-too-familiar patterns. During a fight he shot and killed a rival gang member, for which he served 26 years. "It's sad that two young African-American under-privileged youth played out this scenario," he wrote later. "It happens almost every day in the United States. One goes to his grave and the other to the penitentiary. It's horrible. It's something I'll never get over."

The first years in prison, Jerry was angry and, like many, "learned a whole lot more criminal skills in prison than I had outside." He was regularly in and out of solitary confinement. After five years, he de-cided to change course.

His first influences were Rebels who took the time to mentor and educate him—grandfathers from the Black Panthers and Black Guer-rilla Family. From these elders Jerry learned to see his own life choic-es as part of a larger structure. In reading and discussing, he saw his story as a reflection of patterns. He was responsible for his own choices, but his options were restricted and shaped by systems much bigger than himself—systems of poverty, racism, and exploitation that meant there weren't jobs in his neighborhood, or intervention programs, or family wealth to help him through the hard times. Re-bels' direct and tough talk moved him, despite his own anger and frustrations.

"For me it was infuriating, because I had to learn about the degra-dations that my people went through…. [I learned that the] enemy was not whites or Mexicans, it was the structure, the system that had created slavery and bondage and poverty." Jerry was understanding a key part of movement-building, seeing the world not only through the eyes of individual responsibility, but as a larger structure that needed to be changed, too. An awakening was afoot.

Helpers offered spiritual guidance in dealing with his anger and feelings of hopelessness and powerlessness. "It brought me back to my Christian beliefs.... I had to realize that, again, I didn't have to control everything. Some things I just had to submit to. So, as an example, you've got this guy, he just has to walk on *this* side of the compound when we come out, this is his part: OK, respect that. 'You have it, it's your space, brother.' But coming from a position as a gang member inside prison, from a leadership position this wasn't so easy a lot of times, because now people started to question where my loyalties lay. To do it subtly, as I thought I was going to initially, is not easy: you're not given that kind of space and time in prison by the administration or by your peers. So I had to just be straightforward, cold turkey, 'I'm through with this, this is how I'm living now, don't bring that to me.' After a while people started to respect me for that position."

He joined a victim-offender group, drawing from the restorative justice model.[12] The group, run by Advocates, prepared prisoners to speak with their victims or their victims' surviving relatives. It's a tremendous alternative to the dehumanizing practices of the current criminal justice system. People speak to each other, take responsibility, and help make "right relationships" by supporting healing for all involved.

For Jerry, that program made a huge difference. "When I go to court I'm no longer Jerry Elster, it's the State of California against the defendant. Everything is geared toward dehumanizing. The person who was assaulted or fell prey to this crime is not that person no more, they're the victim of the crime or the plaintiff. I didn't violate the rights of any individual. I violated the rights of the state. So what [the victim-offender group] was able to do was to humanize that process again."

Jerry had moved from thinking individually to structurally—and as good as those steps were, he wasn't satisfied. In his words, the group "helps individuals move forward with accepting their accountability, but it doesn't help the system or society move forward with theirs. There's torture going on in prison, but [they're] not going to sit the warden down or the staff and tell them you got to be more accountable with how you're dealing with people from a restorative justice approach. It says the system's flawed but it doesn't hold the system accountable."

For that, Jerry needed to find groups who were waging campaigns to change the system. He needed to join with others to solve problems and take on the system. "A lot of people get caught up trying to build a campaign without a group. We talk about issues and assume people will automatically come together to resolve that issue. They don't. We have to plug people into groups."[13] And that's when he met other Organizers.

After a talk he gave about his own story, an organizer with All of Us or None came up to him. She heard his story and was moved, and encouraged him to join their group, which had just launched a new campaign to eliminate the box on employment forms asking about prior convictions.

He threw himself into the campaign and joined All of Us or None and a raft of other groups, including the American Friends Service Committee. They lost some campaigns, like a bill against shackling of pregnant women in prison, which was vetoed by the California governor. They won others, like the "Ban the Box" campaign.

Each step Jerry took was supported by different roles: Rebels' tough talk about structural oppression, Helpers assisting his personal growth to take more responsibility, Advocates creating alternative models, and Organizers connecting him with others trying to change the system.

Understanding the different roles in social change helps us see that we each have a special part to play.[14] That part may shift with changing circumstances. Sometimes we'll play multiple parts simultaneously. But strong movements always include a mix of many roles. To craft a movement to eliminate the cycle of caste in the US, including its current form of mass incarceration, we need all of us playing our roles well.

NEXT STEPS

1. What role(s) are you drawn to in movement work? What's a personal strength you bring to that role? What's a challenge you frequently experience in that role?

2. When do you experience conflict or tension with the other roles? What bothers you about them? What are you learning from this chapter that can help you minimize tensions when working with the other roles?

3. Is there a person or organization from a different role that would be strategic for you to build a relationship with? What would be a first step toward building that relationship? How could the different approaches from your roles complement each other?

4. In your group, you may want to introduce these four roles and have people cluster to see where they identify. In coalition meetings or groups, it can help ease tensions between the roles to see them in the open like this. Where might you introduce the four roles as a tool to help a group work better together?

Get more information on the four roles in social change at: www.NewJimCrowOrganizing.org.

CHAPTER 2
BUILDING STRONG GROUPS

Tina Reynolds was arrested for the last time in 1993. After years of cycling in and out of prison, her final prison experience was the most brutal. When she was four-and-a-half months pregnant, guards shackled her ankles, belly, and arms on the hour-and-a-half bus trip to Bedford Hills Correctional Facility for Women. She had to lean on a bar to hold herself up, worrying what might happen to her baby if the bus accidentally bumped the wrong way.[15]

Though often unnoticed by people on the outside, black and brown women are the fastest growing population within the criminal justice system—and about 6 percent of them are pregnant when incarcerated.[16] Through her pregnancy Tina was forced to endure a host of indignities, not the least of which was being denied adequate medical care and enough food to feed her growing fetus. When her water broke she was handcuffed, shackled, and taken to the hospital. Guards kept shackles on her ankles throughout childbirth until the last minute—then swiftly put them back on along with handcuffs while she held her newborn son. She describes this as "the most egregious, dehumanizing, oppressive practice that I ever experienced while in prison."[17]

Tina's story is a powerful indictment of the current system and its lack of humanity. Movements grow from these stories—and Tina had the courage to share hers and encourage others to do the same.

Together with another colleague whose child's father was imprisoned, she founded Women on the Rise Telling Her Story (WORTH). She describes that experience: "We came to the conclusion that our voices were missing from policy conversations about issues facing incarcerated or formerly incarcerated women and their families. Soon enough, people started asking me to speak and join in on the conversation, and other women who had been in jail or prison joined me as well. We all became part of the solution, stood up to represent women in the system and the challenges they face."

Building a group gave them power and a way to create space for women to offer one another mutual support. "While this is about reproductive justice as a human rights issue, it also focuses on the resistance of women behind bars and their ability to lead legislative change after incarceration," she says of WORTH. Buoyed by each other's stories, WORTH decided to target New York prisons' practice of shackling women during childbirth. In 2009 they won that campaign—the first of many policy changes their work has generated.

Individually, Tina Reynolds' story is heartbreaking. Combined with other women's stories, it became a source of outrage that helped channel others into a strong group to make change. Forming such groups gives us strength to tell our stories and have those stories make a difference.

There are many different structures for movement groups. They can be service organizations, nonprofit entities, support groups, religious-based committees, friends who get together, and more. Each structure presents different advantages and disadvantages (and whole books are devoted to this subject[18]). But what they all share is an ability to act courageously together, grow and recruit new people into their fold, and exert their power to make change.

Unfortunately, when many of us think of powerful historical movements, we think of heroic individuals. We've been fed an image of movements that is individualistic. In fact, relationships, especially groups, are the building blocks of movements.

THE MYTH OF ROSA PARKS

Most of us think of Rosa Parks as an individual heroine and changemaker, but a lot of network- and group-building was done before and after Rosa Parks' refusal to give up her seat on the bus. Four days after the landmark 1954 *Brown v. Board of Education* decision, which made separate public schools for blacks and whites illegal, Montgomery, Alabama activist Jo Ann Robinson penned a letter to the mayor on behalf of her organization, the Women's Political Council. In bold Rebel style, she urged the mayor to address the unfair treatment of blacks on city buses, threatening, "There has been talk from 25 or more local organizations of planning a city-wide boycott of buses." Nothing immediate came of that threat.

The next year, a young black woman named Claudette Colvin was arrested for refusing to give up her seat to a white patron on a bus. She contacted well-known Montgomery activist E.D. Nixon, president of the local NAACP and a leader in the Brotherhood of Sleeping Car Porters union. Nixon talked about the situation with Jo Ann Robinson.

They felt that Claudette Colvin wasn't a good rallying point to challenge the system. Nixon thought she was unsuitable to the black community because she fought with and swore at the police (and they later learned she was an unwed, pregnant 15-year-old). Robinson was concerned about her instability and worried that she would break apart under harsh backlash and the pressure of a court case. Their decision was cemented when several of the black witnesses showed signs of backtracking on their story, making any court win unlikely.

These were hard choices to make—and harder a few months later when another woman, Mary Louise Smith, was arrested for the same defiance. She was uneducated, dirt poor, and the daughter of an alcoholic. She was also collected and clear-headed. Robinson said they should press forward.

Nixon said no. He was worried that the black community would not rally strongly to her defense, leaving her abandoned and without the backing to persevere through a grueling fight. He was thinking strategically, knowing that a successful campaign would need to mobilize both the poor black community and the polished middle-class community, who were highly concerned about image and status.

Robinson stewed at the decision. She didn't see those as adequate reasons to keep someone from being a spokesperson.

Do we promote people to leadership who will be "acceptable"? This question is of critical importance to the movement to end mass incarceration and often represents a tough question. Because of the stigma associated with those society has deemed "criminals," it can be tempting to categorize potential leaders according to an external hierarchy of "innocence." We can easily replicate social injustice by promoting people who look mainstream, rather than those who sit on the social margins.

As a case in point, consider CeCe McDonald, a transgender woman who was put in prison after she allegedly killed a man who had shouted racial and transphobic epithets at her and slashed her face, causing her to need eleven stitches. As George Zimmerman's story of killing Trayvon Martin hit newsstands, CeCe's self-defense against a hate crime landed her in prison, sentenced to 41 months in a men's facility without the hormones she would need—another unnoticed tragic story.

An article for Ebony.com was aptly titled: "Why Aren't We Fighting for CeCe McDonald?"[19] The answer: she was a transgender black woman. And such is the challenge for this movement—to raise ourselves above individual cases and proclaim what CeCe proclaimed when she was asked about her experience as a transgender person. "Prisons aren't safe for anyone," she replied, "and that's the key issue."[20]

It's worth emphasizing that neither Nixon nor Robinson used "the public," white citizenry, or the mayor as their yardstick. They wanted to find someone whose cause was righteous, who could withstand the inevitable backlash, and whose story would mobilize *their* constituency. Like good movement players, they were thinking: *What will activate our network and move them into bolder action?*

This takes us to the night Rosa Parks was arrested, after her now-famous refusal to move to the back of the bus. In the police station, she called her mother. A black woman getting arrested in 1955 in Montgomery was trouble. Distraught, her mother immediately called E.D. Nixon to bail her out.

Nixon sprang into action. He first tried to reach black attorney Fred Gray. He left messages all over the city but was unable to find him. So Nixon called the police station. The white desk sergeant refused to speak with him. Growing desperate, he sought out Clifford and Virginia Durr, two white allies who had helped previous organizing efforts. Together the three of them rushed to the police station and bailed out Rosa Parks.

Nixon immediately saw in Rosa Parks the ideal case to challenge discrimination on city buses. She was from the working class but was an established figure in middle-class circles as well. She was a leader in an NAACP struggle to end the impunity with which white men were raping and abusing black women. This had given her exposure to nonviolent action via training at the Highlander Folk School.[21] She maintained a calm, dignified demeanor that won her the respect of both poor blacks and those of the status-conscious middle class.

Rosa Parks was greeted at home by her anxious mother and husband. Despite their fears, Nixon pressed forward, pulling her aside and asking if she would be willing to challenge the case in court, knowing she might face threats and violence.

She had just been through a scary and humiliating experience. Her family was still in shock. She paused at the prospect of exposing them to retribution and said she'd need their support.

When the family had all gathered, Nixon laid out this opportunity to stand up for the entire black community. Her husband hesitated, thinking (quite realistically) that she might get killed. With great trepidation, they agreed.

Nixon was using relationships to do what Organizers often must: challenge people to act. Nixon cared about the Parks family but was encouraging them to act outside their fears. Like Tina Reynolds of WORTH, Nixon was asking people to take risks that might result in bigger change.

It had already been a full evening—but it wasn't over. Late in the night, attorney Fred Gray finally received Nixon's urgent messages, and he called Rosa Parks and agreed to represent her. Thinking about practical next steps, he called Jo Ann Robinson and filled her in on his conversation with Rosa Parks, unaware of all that Nixon had set up. Blocked from taking action previously, Jo Ann Robinson was not to be held back again and sprang into action.

Here we see the power of the Rebel role at work. Miffed at Nixon's past caution, she didn't wait for approval, consensus, grant funding, or a bureaucracy's rubber stamp. *And*, she was wise enough to have built a group around her. Despite the late hour, she called on her colleagues from the Women's Political Council to sneak into Alabama State College, where she was a professor, for a very last-minute, late-night session.

This meeting was critical. The group finalized a flyer calling for a one-day boycott of the buses. Robinson had already thought through the text and just needed to "borrow" the school's resources to get it on paper. With laborious effort, they made thousands of copies on an old-fashioned hand-cranked mimeograph machine. Defying customs about black women traveling at night, they distributed copies all over Montgomery.

Without that group, the movement never would have flourished.

After this was completed—at 3 a.m.—Robinson called Nixon to fill him in on her plans. She was surprised to find him awake. He'd been thinking along similar lines and was immediately supportive.

The depth of their network showed profoundly the next morning. Robinson's group went door-to-door passing out flyers and doing face-to-face recruitment for the boycott. Nixon made a dozen calls convincing church leaders, including the fresh-faced 25-year-old Reverend Martin L. King Jr., to mobilize their churches for the boycott. That network blossomed into a new movement organization called the Montgomery Improvement Association, which became the public face of the movement.

Without those groups, none of us would ever have heard of Rosa Parks. With them, the bus boycott was launched with over 90% support from the black community.

PRIORITIZE RELATIONSHIP-BUILDING

This story holds a host of important lessons for groups. You can see how each role played a part in movement-building: Advocates (Fred Gray), Rebels (Jo Ann Robinson), Helpers (Clifford and Virginia Durr), and Organizers (E.D. Nixon).

The story blows apart the idea that we must look for an individual hero or single act of bravery. We need a network of activated people. E.D. Nixon used his network to mobilize and helped turn it into a movement group, while Jo Ann Robinson's Women's Political

Council was built for quick action and responsiveness. As is true in movement-building, each group was built on strong relationships.

Other key lessons about building a group include:

- Being connected with people playing different roles—you never know when you may need a good Advocate, Rebel, etc.;
- Being organized—use lists, Facebook, phone trees, or some mechanism to keep track of different people so that, like Jo Ann Robinson, you can rapidly activate them;
- Challenging people to tell their stories boldly—encourage people to share their experience with others, even if that includes taking risk;
- Calling people when you need help—movement-building requires reliance on each other, not taking all the work on ourselves. Like Fred Gray, know what you do well (be Rosa Parks's lawyer) and what others should do (let Jo Ann Robinson design the public actions).

Rather than seeing Rosa Parks as the founder of the Montgomery bus boycott, this story reminds us that movements are built on webs of relationships.

In this movement, it's essential to prioritize relationships—despite the challenges the prison system puts in the way. Working inside and out is challenging and requires steady, patient effort. Letters take a long time to go back and forth. Visits are often prevented or halted arbitrarily. Even if solely organizing on the outside, finding time to meet with people can be challenging with all the other demands. Yet it is necessary. In fact, some groups believe relationships are so important they're willing to go to jail for them.

After years of broken promises to fix immigration by politicians in Washington, DC, a group of young, undocumented immigrants wanted to expose the truth—that the government was maliciously rounding up and deporting tens of thousands of people, often without cause. They were fighting another head on the hydra of mass incarceration.

They chose a highly unusual tactic: *trying* to get sent to immigration detention centers.

Though their status as youth without criminal records made their actual deportation less likely, they knew they were taking a huge risk.

But they felt the urgent need to build relationships with those facing the harsh consequences of our country's broken immigration system.

By pretending not to speak English, they found their way into detention centers. There they met people trapped by the system, even as the government was publicly claiming they were only deporting people for egregious violations. Fellow detainees were initially reluctant but slowly began to open up with their stories.

The young immigrants provided advice, like telling them not to sign voluntary deportation papers. But most importantly, they made public people's stories, like that of Javier de los Santos. Javier was being ripped from his infant son because he was caught with a broken license-plate light—another way the harsh sentencing of mass incarceration destroys families.

They fed this information to supporters on the outside. Those supporters lined up a lawyer for Javier, raised money for a bond payment, got local media coverage, and organized an online petition. Their efforts eventually won Javier his freedom, and he was reunited with his son—just one of dozens of people they helped free.

Frustrated by the organizing happening on their watch, the jailers unceremoniously released the young immigrants—who promptly went back in so they could continue to organize.

Their commitment to building relationships exposed the current deportation system as arbitrary, destructive to families, and a needless punishment of vulnerable populations. And it has won high regard as a pressure tactic forcing the government to change its policy by exposing the reality of the system. The young activists' sacrifice also highlights Dr. King's point that unearned suffering can be redemptive.

Not every group-building effort needs to be quite so bold. But no matter our method of organizing, we must build relationships widely. To do this, we need to make use of one the most fundamental movement tools: one-on-one conversations.

ORGANIZE ONE-ON-ONE MEETINGS
Ask most people how they got started with a group, and they'll tell you that someone talked to them and asked them to get involved. That simple one-on-one encounter is too often overlooked once we're in a group. We forget the power of reaching out to others.

The basics of one-on-ones are straightforward:

- Find a time to talk with someone;
- Listen to that person to understand where they're coming from; and
- Make a specific ask tailored to who and where they are (for example sign a petition, bring juice to the next meeting, or speak at an upcoming event).

One-on-ones enable a group to grow. Groups wanting to attract new members or participants need to continually meet with new people one-on-one, whether by knocking on doors in a neighborhood, talking on the phone, or shouting through cell walls.

They are also helpful in strengthening groups. Groups are only as strong as the relationships binding them together. Some groups spend too much time in meetings or events, while overlooking the importance of one-on-one and small group time among their members.

During one-on-ones, we can make "asks" of people, inviting them to take on a little more leadership than they have shown before. Southern organizer Si Kahn writes about the difference between general requests ("please help us in whatever way you can") and specific requests, which are more likely to actually recruit someone. During a campaign to close an immigrant family detention center, Si's group made *specific* asks to specific people.

> *Grassroots Leadership invites artists, musicians, and poets to help spread the word about immigrant family detention. What YOU can do:*
> • *Make a brief announcement about the Campaign at your concerts and, where appropriate, pass the hat and send contributions to the Campaign;*
> • *Write and/or record a song about immigrant family detention;*
> • *Put information about the Campaign to End Immigrant Family Detention on your website and in your newsletters;*
> • *Mention the Campaign when you are interviewed on the radio or in other media.*[22]

You need to have a good sense of what tasks people can help with— otherwise, you'll lose the energy of potential volunteers who think you're great but don't know how to plug in. Notice how Si's group didn't just ask folks to come to a meeting, but customized their asks to the people they were asking (musicians/artists/poets). Their requests were specific, tangible, doable, and tailored to their audience.

Gail Tyree is an experienced organizer who uses powerful one-on-ones in her organizing. While sponsored by Grassroots Leadership, she worked on a campaign against a proposed immigrant detention center in Southwest Ranches, Florida. They were against huge forces: a massive explosion of rounding up undocumented immigrants (in 2011, over 420,000 people were placed in detention centers[23]) and the powerful private prison lobby that locks up half of them. "Most people when they're dealing with a situation want to vent about it but they're not really ready to take action," Gail explained. "They need support to really get involved—and that's not easy to do."[24]

One young woman, Ryan Greenberg, lived right across the street from the proposed detention center site. Ryan was reluctant to get involved in the campaign. She told Gail, "I know it's wrong, but I don't have time for this fight. They're gonna win anyway. And I have other things to do."

Gail sat down with Ryan at a sandwich shop. She listened for a long time about Ryan's life, her concerns, her priorities, and all the reasons she felt she couldn't get involved in the campaign. After a while, Gail said, "You don't have to help with this campaign. I can't make you do it. But where your house is located, you're going to be able to see the prison, right down the hill from your back yard. Now imagine your daughter sees some of the immigrant girls down the hill playing and she says, 'There are some girls down the hill mama, Can I play with them?' You tell me, what are you going to tell your daughter? How are you going to explain that these little girls are in prison and did not do anything illegal to be there, in addition you did nothing to stop this place from being built?"

Ryan opened her eyes and immediately broke into tears. Gail joined her, recalling that they cried for ten minutes together. Gail then asked Ryan to join the campaign and come to meetings regularly—which she readily did. Ryan soon became a leader in the campaign and continues to be a voice in her community against immigrant detention centers and for-profit private prisons.

"Whenever she was ready to quit," Gail recalls, "all I had to do was remind her about this conversation and the pain she felt. She was convicted to the cause."

Gail knew that getting people motivated is crucial. "When you're working as an organizer, you're almost like a neighborhood psychologist. You have to help people through their pain. You should spend most of the time listening to the pain." Getting to that point requires listening patiently and closely to people and connecting to their deeper motivations, hopes, and dreams.

RECRUIT PEOPLE OUTSIDE YOUR CIRCLE

Even if they use one-on-ones effectively, many groups reach a point where they stop growing. Such groups often mistakenly believe they've tapped all the people who are passionate about their issue. *"Nobody else cares about solitary confinement or the treatment of families in detention centers."* The problem is often not that we have exhausted the possibilities in our city or small town—it's how we are organizing and the way we think about growing our group.

When it comes to recruitment, many of us think of people just as individuals. We imagine there is a scattering of people out there from whom to recruit (left side of image).

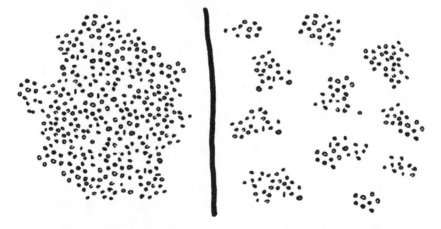

The reality is different. Most people are not attracted to groups as individual entities. Ask around, and you'll find that very few people get involved in a cause because they receive a flyer, get sent an e-mail, see a poster, or see a Facebook post. Most people join a group or get involved because someone they know personally invited them.

That's because society is better understood as clusters of "social circles" (right side of image).

Social circles may be organized as formal or informal groups—religious communities, gangs, tight-knit neighborhoods, etc. If you happen to be on Facebook, you can see your social circle by the number of people who are friends of friends many times over.

The quickest way to build a group is to ask people in your networks of friends or family. Those people are the most likely to say yes to you. But a group stops growing when it reaches its maximum potential of people from its members' initial social circle. Continuing to reach out within that circle may not bring in many more people. The trick is to jump out of your social circle and find people connected with other social circles.

Some ways to do this:

- *Show up at the events and meetings of people outside your circle*—it's a great chance to meet others, see how they work, and find out where their values overlap with your campaign;
- *Stop doing the tactics you've always been doing and try new ones that might appeal to different audiences*—if your tactics are marches, vigils, or standing outside of prisons during executions and it's not working, then it's time to adapt. Ritualizing our actions makes us predictable and boring. People want to join fresh and interesting groups;
- *Notice when other groups make overtures toward your movement, and follow up with them*—for example, in response to the Michael Brown slaying in Ferguson, Missouri, a leading climate change organization, 350.org, made a public statement against police militarization.[25] This kind of overture deserves someone reaching out to them to find out what inspired the move and what it would take to build stronger alignment;
- *Do lots of one-on-ones with leaders from other movements and groups*—meet with different people, not to recruit them but to learn from them. *What are their values? What interests them? What strategies recruit people like them?*
- *Do direct service*—Gandhi was a big fan of what he called the "constructive program," which means not only campaigning against what we don't want but also building the alternative that

we do want (a natural role for Helpers). Direct service and other community-based projects put us shoulder to shoulder with others who want to make things better. Who better to hear a pitch about joining your campaign?

Growing outside of your social circle takes time, but when it comes to building successful groups, it's worth the effort.

DEVELOP A SHARED POWER ANALYSIS

Once you have a group of people, the challenge is figuring out what to do with it. It's helpful to spend time developing a shared analysis of how your group has power to make change.

Unfortunately, like other myths put out there, the dominant view of power isn't pro-social change. The dominant view is that power flows from the top downward. A janitor takes orders from a supervisor who takes orders from a district head, and so on—all the way up to, say, a CEO or the president of the United States at the very top of the pyramid.

Most institutions in our society are viewed this way. In terms of prisons, you might see the state governor near the top. They pick a warden, who selects a deputy warden, who oversees the shift commander, who gives orders to guards, and so on, with prisoners way down at the bottom. In that view of society, everyone below has to follow orders or face consequences: be fired, jailed, or put in solitary.

But there's another way of helping groups view power: the upside-down triangle.

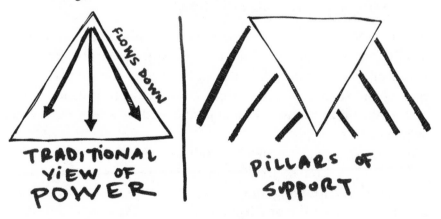

TRADITIONAL VIEW OF POWER

PILLARS OF SUPPORT

An upside-down triangle is inherently unstable. An oppressive system that relies on abusing and degrading humans is insecure—it requires being held up by *pillars of support*. Some of those pillars include social systems that give the structure legitimacy, such as laws, courts, the media, and schools that train us to obey. Other pillars include people who may oppose the system but are complicit in keeping it running—including administrators, guards, chaplains, janitors, construction workers who build prisons, and so on.

This view of power helps reveal how much agency we actually have. The most repressive mayor is powerless if citizens refuse to pay taxes. The most racist bus system cannot keep up its racist practices if its customer base refuses to ride the buses. The cruelest warden is forced to come to the negotiating table when prisoners refuse to eat.

Groups can use this tool to look at their work and develop a more complex and accurate analysis of power. Identifying the *pillars of support* that keep bad policies in place can help expand our sense of how we can make change.

Fighting against an entrenched and ruthless dictator in Serbia, one group of activists explains this power analysis this way:

> By themselves, rulers cannot collect taxes, enforce repressive laws and regulations, keep trains running on time, prepare national budgets, direct traffic, manage ports, print money, repair roads, keep food supplied to the markets, make steel, build rockets, train the police and the army, issue postage stamps or even milk a cow. People provide these services to the ruler through a variety of organizations and institutions. If the people stop providing these skills, the ruler cannot rule.[26]

They believed this so deeply that they required every movement member to get training in which they identified pillars of support in their society and designed strategies to remove those pillars. That training and shared approach was a key ingredient in their massive movement, which successfully and nonviolently overthrew the brutal Serbian dictator.[27]

Bringing this power analysis to our networks grows our understanding of structural oppression, including the ways that our shame, our silence, our willful ignorance, our refusal to take risks, and our turning away from the problem all have a part to play. It brings us face to face with the reality of *our* power—challenging our group to consider whether and how we are putting that power to use.

This is one of the key insights from nonviolent direct action. Rather than seeing power as flowing from violence or exploitation, groups come to see that power flows through relationships and that we surrender our power whenever we remain complicit in unjust relationships.

A campaign from the 1970s illustrates this. The US government was sending weapons to Pakistani dictator Yahya Khan that were used to murder the people of East Pakistan (now Bangladesh). In an attempted genocide, nearly 3 million East Pakistanis were killed.

A group of Philadelphia, Pennsylvania Quakers wanted to make a difference. When they found out that some of the arms shipments were loaded from local Philadelphia ports, they picked a dramatic action to stop the flow of weapons: a naval blockade! For a month, they publicly practiced "naval maneuvers" in canoes and kayaks in front of TV cameras. Some days had themes—religious leaders, kids, elders—all leading up to the arrival of the gigantic multistory freighter ships bound for Pakistan.

When the first ship arrived, the group jumped into the water with their canoes and paddle boats. The coast guard immediately pulled them out, as camera operators angled for the best picture. Over the next weeks, they played a cat-and-mouse game, as the freighters tried to avoid the public spotlight by changing their arrival times or rerouting to Baltimore, Maryland or New York City. But an important group of people was watching the unfolding storyline on TV: the longshoremen employed to load the ships.

The Quakers went to bars and met with them. The longshoremen were struck by their sincerity and the sense that this was a historic moment. The Philadelphia union agreed to refuse to load armaments headed to Pakistan. It was the beginning of the end.

Philly longshoremen convinced the national union to cease loading any military shipments to Pakistan. With that crucial pillar of support removed, the government couldn't use any port on the East Coast to send arms. This classic civil disobedience made it prohibitively expensive to send the weapons. Soon after, the federal government announced it would no longer support the dictator (and, unsurprisingly, did not mention the activists' role).[28]

Without firing a shot or making a single lobby visit, this small group forced the hand of the largest empire the world has known. That's power.

Groups will be well-served by using the upside-down triangle. It gets us thinking about the pillars we can remove, which helps us to see our own power. Groups can easily run themselves down by focusing on what they can't do and the people they can't save. Losing sight of our agency and where we can make a difference can sink our groups into despair.

Susan Burton, a formerly incarcerated woman who runs A New Way of Life, a comprehensive re-entry program in California, has offered one striking example of how the mass incarceration movement might topple a key pillar of support.[29] She's noted that the vast majority of people in the court system take plea bargains—about 90%. This is a practical and rational choice, even if they are innocent, rather than risk the harsh sentencing of mandatory minimums.

The old view of power looks at this and sees people trapped in the system, powerless in the face of district attorneys and mandatory minimums. Yet Susan's "crash the system" tactic could flip the script and remove our collusion with the system: *Instead of accepting plea bargains, large numbers of people collectively demand their constitutional right to a jury of their peers.*

Such an action could indeed crash the system, which is already overloaded. The courts need people accepting plea bargains to function smoothly. In that way, the system depends on the cooperation of the oppressed.

Imagine how this might play out: In a small city, 100 people refuse to accept plea bargains. They collectively demand jury trials. The already stretched and overloaded city judiciary scrambles to arrange jury trials. Those who are unable (or who refuse) to pay their bond are stuck in jails. (This tactic, as any to shift a system this huge, would require suffering.) Others who are released tour the country to rally support.

Hearing about this, a few thousand more join in this "crash the system" tactic. They argue that the system has no intention of supporting their constitutional rights and that it was never designed to do so. Unable to quickly process people, cities fill all their jail beds and flail around to deal with the overwhelming numbers.

People are inspired. Soon tens of thousands across the nation (still a small number overall) refuse plea bargains. Courts around the country grind to a halt as overloaded justice systems cannot accommodate the demands. Supportive lawyers file federal appeals to challenge the courts' inability to implement constitutionally required jury trials. Public protests ensue around the country, demanding immediate release of all those who are being (and were) denied their constitutional right for a trial by a jury of their peers.

The overburdened criminal justice system cannot cope, lacking enough jurors, lawyers, or judges to continue to function. The system falls into chaos.

We could keep imagining. Scrambling, politicians offer minor concessions or try various measures to keep the system afloat. In response, the tens of thousands crashing the system build a sort of "defendants' union," which refuses the minor concessions. The union instead negotiates on behalf of hundreds of thousands for major, fundamental reforms.

Perhaps the negotiations break down, and the "union" calls for a complete change, escalating its goals and tactics in order to remove more pillars of support until radical demands are met. Hunger strikes inside sweep through prisons, people in jail refuse bail so as to occupy beds and further destabilize the system, jurors add pressure by slowing down court proceedings, ally lawyers and public defenders strike until all demands are met, taxpayers refuse to pay taxes, ally guards walk off their jobs, governors are hounded until they grant wide immunity, and so on. The system collapses, and the union becomes the leader in a transitional system built on restorative justice principles.

All this because people took big collective risks by removing their cooperation with the system.

The visioning here is important, because without it we dream small and of only the tiniest incremental changes. One activist said it this way: "If I don't believe I have the power to change something, then I won't think about it." Through analyzing our own power using the upside-down triangle, we can help our groups think bigger, recognizing the power we have when we refuse to cooperate with the system as it currently functions.

ELIMINATE THE SMOG INSIDE US

Despite our best efforts and educational work, all of us have internalized some of the oppression inflicted by the prison industrial complex. Whoever we are, we've internalized some of the lessons taught by this system of racialized mass incarceration, about dehumanizing the lives of people of color and discounting the ill-treatment of people in jails and prisons, along with an ingrained instinct for retributive justice or inferiority for who we are.

Some have likened oppression to smog. Without a choice, we all inhale smog. It is in our body. The toxicity of oppression is in each and every one of us. It makes us callous to the oppression of others—and even our own selves. We must detoxify ourselves, eliminating those beliefs that make prisons okay or that grind away at our sense of self-worth. We must detoxify ourselves from the smog and create a culture that stands on higher principles.

For example, following the high-profile killing of Trayvon Martin and the subsequent protests, the Ella Baker Center for Human Rights published an article challenging those of us calling for his killer's prosecution: "Justice for Trayvon Martin: Why Punishing His Killer Isn't Enough."[30] In it they pointed out that the state enacting violence against Trayvon's killer would not create justice and certainly would not address the underlying racism that allows black people's lives to be treated so cavalierly. Responding individually to a social problem will not fix it.

This article calls us back to deeper values—away from a focus on the *laws* being broken to the *harm* being done. "In our current legal system, there are no meaningful spaces or processes for this kind of accountability. Instead, a retributive justice system like ours offers only blame, punishment, and reinforcement of power hierarchies."

In the wake of additional killings, others have similarly encouraged us to turn away from a system of retributive violence and consider alternative processes, like Truth and Reconciliation commissions.[31]

Getting the smog of out of our systems is not an individual task. We need to do it together. We need each other's help so that we're removing the many layers of human degradation—another reason for us to work across issues and draw connections between race, class, gender, sexual orientation, immigration status, and the many other ways that society divides us up.

The late Eddie Ellis described how language shapes our public perception of people, like himself, who were incarcerated:

> *When we are not called mad dogs, animals, predators, offenders and other derogatory terms, we are referred to as inmates, convicts, prisoners and felons—all terms devoid of humanness which identify us as 'things' rather than as people. These terms are accepted as the 'official' language of the media, law enforcement, prison industrial complex and public policy agencies.... In an effort to assist our transition from prison to our communities as responsible citizens and to create a more positive human image of ourselves, we are asking everyone to stop using these negative terms and to simply refer to us as PEOPLE. People currently or formerly incarcerated, PEOPLE on parole, PEOPLE recently released from prison, PEOPLE in prison, PEOPLE with criminal convictions, but PEOPLE.[32]*

His open letter encouraged all groups to switch to that new language. This is akin to the immigration rights movement, which convinced the Associated Press to refuse to call people "illegal immigrant" and instead use the phrase "undocumented residents."

Our groups likewise need to engage in such self-reflection. Removing the smog is not easy, but to bring about a stronger society rooted in human values, we have to carve out space for that work. Ongoing anti-racism and undoing oppression educational and training opportunities can help us get rid of the smog inside of us.[33]

EMPOWER LEADERSHIP FROM THE OPPRESSED

In many social movements, women do 80% of the work, while 80% of leadership positions are held by men.[34] Such a disproportionate ratio holds true for many other historically oppressed groups—people of color, gays and lesbians, transgender people, and, most certainly, formerly incarcerated people and their families.

There's a natural power struggle between people in the prison justice system, their friends and families, and those who are allies but not directly impacted. That is a challenge for this movement. *Should incarcerated and formerly incarcerated people and their families lead the movement, or should it be led by allies? Who determines its direc-*

tion, priorities, and tactics? Those from oppressed groups bring a sense of urgency and energy, while, generally speaking, groups led by "allies" have more traditional resources but tend to be more cautious.

This is common in movements. "The anti-Vietnam War movement, for example, increased its energy and militancy when draft-age youths took leadership," wrote some movements activists. "In 1963, largely conventional tactics were used by peace organizations, even in the face of Vietnamese monks burning themselves in protest. When Students for a Democratic Society called the first mass rally in Washington in 1966, the movement shifted into a higher gear both in analysis and tactics."[35]

Allies may bring financial resources, formal education, and a range of passions and backgrounds that can be of great assistance. With their self-confidence and excitement to share, they can quickly step into leadership roles—often at the expense of leadership of directly impacted people. Even if there's not a take-over of leadership, allies might dampen a group's progress by urging caution rather than action.

One way this dynamic often plays out is in the difference between national organizations—which tend to be led by allies—and local groups, often led by directly impacted people.

Take the stream of the black freedom struggle. Before the 1960s, when what we now call the civil rights movement came to a boil, there was a great deal of local experimentation with tactics and strategy. In the 1930s, '40s, and '50s, new tactics were originated and tried out. Some—like early sit-in campaigns—were initially successful. Others—like a wave of initial "freedom rides"—had to be aborted because of extreme violence. Those early experiments were mostly tried by local groups led by people with a powerful sense of urgency, long before the national movement adopted those tactics and ran with them. Even a prototype of the famous March on Washington was attempted in 1941, by union leader A. Philip Randolph. Randolph's mere threat of organizing thousands of black people to descend on Washington, DC so unnerved President Roosevelt that he agreed to prohibit racial discrimination in the national defense industry. All the while, the more privileged NAACP provided local groups with expertise and legal defense, but was more risk averse. Its national prominence drew funding that might otherwise have gone to local initiatives.

Rev. Kenneth Glasgow, a member of the steering committee of the Formerly Incarcerated and Convicted People's Movement (FICPM), describes this dynamic: "When you have these national groups that overshadow or capitalize off work that we have done as grassroots, the funding goes to them. It never makes it to the hard-down person that just got out of prison, that can't get a job, can't get a house, can't get a business license, and is out there struggling and passing out fliers, and looking for a stipend, but we can't give him a stipend because the grant money done went somewhere else."[36]

National groups are rarely at the forefront of bold experimentation. Creativity, risk-taking, and ingenuity need to be unshackled from worries about national reputation, concerned donors, or ensconced stakeholders. In fact, local groups often have to carve out space away from national organizations, which can be destructive when they attempt to dictate "the" strategy for change to the grassroots.

In the past several years, as the movement to end mass incarceration has grown and more ally groups have emerged, there is increasing need to identify and strengthen leaders coming from inside the oppressive system. Groups like the FICPM have arisen to network such leaders and provide cohesive, visionary leadership for the movement. They explain:

> *Efforts to convene formerly-incarcerated people are not new, and we have been a part of most of such efforts over the last ten years. But most of these previous efforts – including the most resourced amongst them – largely unraveled, failed or otherwise erupted into factional battles and infighting. Sometimes these efforts failed because they were directed or otherwise guided by foundations or national advocacy groups without the meaningful involvement of, or formal direction or guidance by, formerly-incarcerated people themselves. And sometimes these efforts failed because formerly-incarcerated people themselves did not have, and did not build, the right spaces and processes for such a convening to occur – we did not have the opportunity to gather and work out critical questions, debates, contradictions and problems necessary to generate a stronger foundation to build upon. The national gatherings we call for now must, both in practice and perception, be organized by formerly-incarcerated*

people, and there must be ample space to work to resolve questions, problems and issues that have divided us in the past. We must assume the lead and control the process and direction.[37]

To support that process, groups must keep asking how to empower and develop leadership from the people most impacted by mass incarceration. As we do that, we'll be in better shape to run powerful, effective campaigns.

NEXT STEPS

1. This chapter highlights the importance of building groups and networks. Take a moment to list your own relationships with individuals or groups that could be helpful to your movement. Think beyond just the people or groups who already come to your meetings, protests, or events. Who else is impacted by the issues you're working on?

2. Looking at your list of relationships, who are you already close to? Who do you have less connection to? How can you use one-on-ones to strengthen your relationships? Choose five or more individuals that would be beneficial to do one-on-ones with.

3. How could a concept like the upside-down triangle be helpful to your groups? What could your group learn from exploring it together? What are some ways you could introduce the upside-down triangle or other power analyses in your groups?

4. Eliminating the smog inside of us is a helpful metaphor as we think about recovering our own humanity, free from the lessons the current system inflicts on us. What are some ways you see the toxic smog inside of you? What are ways you can help reclaim your own humanity? How can members of your group support each other in this difficult and essential work to get rid of the smog inside of each other?

5. How can you use an upcoming event that your group is doing to cultivate leadership by people who are most impacted? What are the leadership tasks and roles you can invite people to step into?

Get instructions on leading the upside-down triangle activity at: www.NewJimCrowOrganizing.org.

CHAPTER 3
CREATING EFFECTIVE CAMPAIGNS

In September 2011, the state of Georgia put Troy Davis to death despite a compelling case of innocence. Protests echoed around the country and globe. Six months later, Trayvon Martin was shot and killed by George Zimmerman. Again, mass protests around the country highlighted the injustice of police bias and Florida's notorious stand-your-ground law that found Zimmerman not guilty. On the heels of that, the persistent miscarriage of justice was highlighted when a black woman, Marissa Alexander—in the same state with the same prosecutor—was given 20 years for shooting a warning shot in the direction of her abusive husband. He was not injured.

Five months later, police in California shot unarmed 25-year-old Manuel Diaz as he fled police. The next day, police in the same city shot and killed another Latino, Joel Acevedo, under questionable circumstances. A little over a year later in Ferguson, Missouri, a police officer fired six shots into the body of Michael Brown, a young black man who according to witnesses held his hands above his head shouting, "I don't have a gun, stop shooting!"

These are just a few of the many cases of open, brutal violence by the state. After many incidents the community mobilizes, taking to the street and marching to express outrage. In some cases, the news gains national attention, such as in Ferguson. There, marches went late into the night, with escalated violence from the police, who were more heavily armed than some US soldiers in Afghanistan.

These protests are important in bringing to light what many in black, brown, and poor communities already know—how rapidly state violence can escalate. These events expose the myth that racism ended with the election of a black president. Instead, more people see that the portrayal of black (and increasingly Latino) people as violent thugs results in twitchy police who fire multiple shots into the bodies of people at the slightest breath of provocation.[38] Then a whole system, from governors, mayors, district attorneys, and police chiefs to armed-to-the-teeth police, protects and colludes, covering up and disguising state-sanctioned violence.

These kinds of protests need to continue—and they are not enough to make change. They are correct and proper defensive responses of communities under attack. But a movement that stays on the defensive will never achieve its goals.

After each cry of "Never again!" the system has remained relatively unscathed. Those at the top wait until the heat blows over. Georgia's death penalty remains in place. Florida considers *expanding* its shoot-to-kill laws. Police involved in slayings return to duty. Protests slowly ebb away as the immediate outrage fades.

These protest responses will continue to increase as more people become conscious, angry, and aware. However, unless we can direct our energy from reactive to proactive, we will be stuck on the defensive. Instead of adapting to the timeline of the courts, the board of pardon and paroles, or the police department's internal investigations, we need to create our own timeline that allows us to keep building pressure and power.

To do that, we need to learn the art of campaigning.

WHAT IS A CAMPAIGN?
Groups often squander precious energy on a series of endless educational events or support groups that don't seem to add up to anything. In contrast, campaigns channel group power by focusing on a concrete goal.

Rather than focusing on the problems of society, campaigns identify a piece of what we want and work toward achieving it. Having such a goal strengthens educational events, support services, and protests. After those events, people are immediately offered additional actions to take—which help them see their power to make change. Thus, campaigns inspire people into further action and help them understand the depth of the problem—both of which increase a group's capacity.

ENDLESS ACTIONS

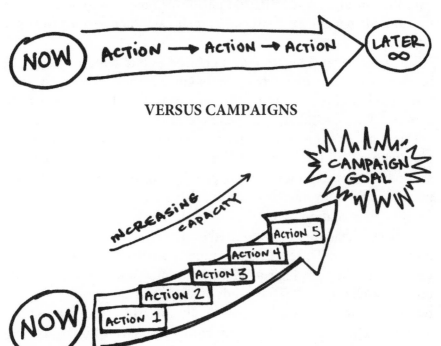

VERSUS CAMPAIGNS

Laurie Jo Reynolds was part of a loose group of people who wanted to do something about mass incarceration. Their informal club, the Tamms Poetry Committee, sent poems to imprisoned men held in brutal secure housing units in the small town of Tamms, Illinois. At the time, they were not running a campaign—they had no clear objective or outcome. They were spreading good deeds, hoping to somehow catalyze change.

They could have done an endless series of actions with minimal impact—if it hadn't been for the response of incarcerated people like Johnnie Walton. Johnnie received their correspondence and was a bit startled by the seemingly random gesture. As told in *Locked Down, Locked Out: Why Prison Doesn't Work and How We Can Do Better*, he thought, "A poetry committee? Men are mutilating themselves, slitting their wrists here.... What do we need with a poetry committee?"[39] He and others wrote Laurie Jo back and urged their group to work for tangible changes.

Advised by Johnnie and others, the group decided on a specific campaign goal: limiting terms at the horrendous Tamms facility. To win, they needed to identify the person or people who could make the desired change—"the target." In their case, they decided to target legislators.

The group picked tactics that mobilized public sentiment and put pressure on legislators: "vigils, press conferences, lobbying days at the capitol, and a community picnic complete with a parsley-eating contest." They eventually achieved their reform goal.

This led to a common campaign outcome: people wanted more. Men released from Tamms took on leadership in the group. Johnnie and other formerly incarcerated people became spokespeople and leaders in the movement, which escalated its campaign goal to the complete elimination of the Tamms facility.

Achieving that bold goal required escalation and an increase in the group's capacity. The group got Amnesty International to condemn the prison. They got high-profile media interviews with former inmates, which they put in the hands of legislators along with the many reasons to close the facility. Eventually their influence was strong enough that the governor, largely citing cost savings, line-item vetoed the Tamms prison. They won!

This is an example of the power of campaigns. Campaigns are a useful way to make change because they:

- Have specific, defined goals that build momentum and energy, rather than spreading attention across many different actions that don't add up to concrete gains;
- Have a specific "target," the individual or individuals who can make the change, thus focusing limited movement resources;
- Use many different kinds of tactics and actions, offering a range of ways for people to join and participate;
- Increase the effectiveness of educational events by showing how each action builds on previous steps and moves toward the goal;
- Keep up pressure over time in order to win concessions, as opposed to one-time actions that allow the target to simply wait until the storm blows over;

- Build leadership at the grassroots and connect with new allies;
- Take the offensive and build their own timeline for change.

PICK A CAMPAIGN GOAL

Many groups wonder: *What campaign goals should we pick?* The current system of enforcement, imprisonment, and discrimination touches almost all of our lives—and in many ways. There are so many issues to tackle.

Because the system is so expansive, there are a host of campaigns being waged around the country as part of the movement to end mass incarceration. Here are just a few samples among many, many campaigns chipping away at the system:[40]

Stopping prison construction and reducing incarceration rates

- Students, like those in the Philadelphia Student Union, campaign to end the school-to-prison pipeline by organizing for equitable school funding and the reduction of policies that contribute to school violence;
- A network of dozens of groups waged an electoral campaign to pass California's Proposition 47, the Reduced Penalties for Some Crimes Initiative;
- Nationally, groups advocate for the decriminalization of marijuana and other drugs—for example, Drop the Rock Coalition's campaign in New York City to the end Rockefeller drug laws, which required long sentences for the sale or possession of very small amounts of drugs;
- The Ella Baker Center and others have run successful campaigns closing individual youth prisons in California, with an eye to stop youth prisons entirely;
- Youth Art & Self-Empowerment Project runs a campaign to repeal Act 33, a harsh Pennsylvania law that broadened the number of youth sent to adult prisons.

Prison conditions

- Prison Phone Justice works to end the outrageous rates that incarcerated people pay for phone calls—as high as $8.40 for a 15-minute call;

- The National Religious Campaign Against Torture and many other groups campaign to end or curtail the use of solitary confinement;
- Birthing Behind Bars campaigns nationally to stop the shackling of pregnant women (in addition to other reproductive justice goals);
- Locked Up and #ShippedAway aims to end Vermont's practice of shipping imprisoned people out of state—a practice that benefits for-profit private prisons.

Ending re-entry barriers and increasing direct services
- A great many organizations, including Jericho Reentry Program and A New Way of Life Reentry Project, run campaigns to increase government funding for a full range of services for people coming out of prison;
- Justice Silence fights for recognition in the justice system for people who are deaf or hard of hearing;
- TakeAction Minnesota drove a three-year campaign to convince Target to "ban the box";
- The National Voting Rights Campaign, run by FICPM, aims to assist formerly incarcerated people and families in registering to vote.

Contributing structural issues
- Jobs Not Jails in Massachusetts built a coalition of a hundred organizations to persuade their governor to agree to no new prisons in the state and is working to move the money saved into "creating good jobs in low-income, high-crime neighborhoods";
- Seeing the need for building financial power for economically marginalized groups, the Southern Grassroots Economies Project creates local co-ops, which helps build self-reliance among poor and immigrant communities;
- In contrast to the increased militarization of schools (for example, metal detectors and bars on windows), schools are eliminating detectors and instead teaching students, teachers, and administrators non-coercive, nonviolent responses to conflict—as taught by groups like the Alternatives to Violence Project;[41]

- The Prison Policy Initiative is a legal resource for incarcerated and formerly incarcerated people with a special focus on mental health, urging policy changes in a system where people with mental health conditions constitute 64% of the jail population.

Alternatives to incarceration
- The Neighborhood Restorative Justice Program in the Ninth District of Florida and Restorative Justice for Oakland Youth are two examples of many restorative justice programs offering an alternative to the current system, even in the case of murder;[42]
- Homeboy Industries is an example of a group hiring people out of prison, providing job skills training, like training people to install solar panels;
- The Audre Lorde Project is a Lesbian, Gay, Bisexual, Two Spirit, Trans and Gender Non-Conforming People of Color organizing center that has multiple campaigns, including a Safe OUTside the System (SOS) Collective which prevents hate and police violence using community-based strategies, like teaching businesses alternative responses to violence other than calling law enforcement.

Groups are often overwhelmed by the array of issues that the movement faces and wonder which will lead to the greatest impact. *How to select among the many injustices and practices that are devastating our communities and families?*

It can be tempting to avoid focusing our energy anywhere and opt for educational work or doing a little of everything. Yet single events can be easily ignored. The power of campaigns comes from using pressure over time to make a target change their position.

Picking one campaign issue doesn't mean we stop talking and thinking about the other issues—in fact, quite the opposite. While focusing on a single goal, groups can connect their campaign to other issues and movements. We all should think deeply and widely about the intersection of mass incarceration and mass deportation, for example, and between class-based oppression and gender- or sexuality-based oppression. In an organization I worked with, we developed an activity called the "newspaper game." We would open up the newspaper and read articles to each other and then practice describing how our campaign was connected to that issue. It developed our skill in being able to connect our issue to anyone and any-thing—and helped us politicize our group's members so they could make connections to other issues, too.

Different groups pick campaign goals differently. A helpful story comes from All of Us or None, a group that is nationally known for spurring "Ban the Box" campaigns. Linda Evans, one of the co-founders, describes their start. "The first real embodiment of All of Us or None was a statewide strategy session that happened in Oak-land in the beginning of March [2003]. We invited almost 50 former prisoners who were organizers from around the state of California to come together and develop a strategy that would be a statewide strat-egy."[43]

The invited organizers had spent time in immigrant detention cen-ters, county jails, federal and state prisons, and juvenile halls. Over half were women, 90% were people of color, and one-third were un-der the age of 23. The intention from the start was clear, as co-founder Dorsey Nunn explains: "It was a strategy session. It was the first time that we brought former prisoners into the room and said we need to talk to each other—and we did that across age, across race, across geography. It was the first time that we asked 'What's good for us?' and spoke with our own voice. We have the power to decide where we go with a struggle that we're developing."

They wanted to acknowledge the spiritual component of this work and so started "with a Native American prayer and followed by pass-ing around a candle which I brought from Africa." They then asked people to discuss the issues that were impacting their communities: California's three strikes law, the deportation of juveniles away from their families, barriers to re-entry and employment, and so on.

Next, they used a big piece of newsprint to help assess people's en-ergy for working on different issues. On it, they listed issues. Each person was given three dots and was asked to put a dot next to issues they wanted to focus on—a kind of voting system. (This is a process sometimes called "dotocracy.")

That helped the group identify a loose sense of direction. For ex-ample, many dots were clustered around barriers to re-entry and dis-crimination against formerly incarcerated people.

This marked the first broad sweep. But, like most groups, they didn't create a new campaign all at once.

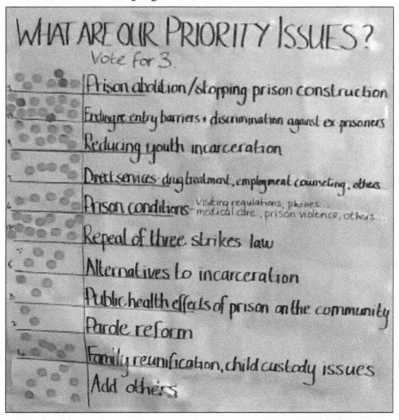

Those issues needed to find expression in specific campaign goals. Dorsey, Linda, and others headed to a national conference organized by Critical Resistance in New Orleans to do what organizers do: bring people together. Dorsey and crew shared their intentions with over 50 national activists, all of whom were formerly incarcerated people. The activists narrowed the first sweep into three objectives:

- develop a national alliance by and for people in prison, formerly incarcerated people, and their families;
- build political power so they can participate in the political process, locally and nationally;
- eliminate discrimination against people with felony convictions, and fight for the human and civil rights of people in prison, formerly incarcerated people, and their families.

A new civil rights movement organization was being built up from the grassroots.

During that national gathering and subsequent community summits, organizers heard a regular refrain about job and housing discrimination. These barriers are widespread and debilitating to those with a conviction history—and one reason why three out of five formerly incarcerated people remain jobless one year after their release from prison.[44]

If there had been a vibrant national campaign already under way on this issue, All of Us or None may have joined that ongoing effort—but looking around, they didn't find one. Lacking that, they searched for specific campaign goals that would speak to their folks and make a difference.

The process of testing a campaign goal is vital. Many progressive-minded reforms that seem like good ideas may actually worsen problems. For example, in the aftermath of Ferguson, some people asked for more police training. Yet, according to reports, St. Louis police received approximately 5,000 hours of training to "deal with potential unrest."[45] Understanding structural impacts is key to choosing campaign goals that will result in meaningful change. We must therefore look beyond hypothetical or academic thinking and listen to people whose expertise of the system comes through lived experience.

Dorsey explains his process: "When I checked in with people asking how their job searches were going, it was always the same answer: checking 'yes' on that box meant their job application was tossed aside. Then one day when I went to Jack in the Box for lunch, the guy behind the counter had tattoos all over his arms." Dorsey noted they were the same gang tattoos he had seen while visiting Mariona prison in El Salvador. "I asked him how he got this job and found out that Jack in the Box did not ask potential employees about their criminal records."

That inspired him to identify a new goal: to have others join Jack in the Box and "ban the box."

Setting a goal was a step. But it needed another step: selecting who to target to make the change. Campaigns are waged by asking *someone* to do something—change a policy, write a law, stop an action, or create a new system. The people who can make these changes are usually quite happy to avoid doing so, either because they disagree with the change or they'd prefer to pretend it's someone else's responsibility. Change will not happen, therefore, unless the target is faced with direct, persistent pressure. It's therefore crucial to identify the appropriate *target* of the campaign—the person or people who could implement a new policy. In the case of All of Us or None, they needed research in order to decide who to target: *Corporations? Nonprofits? Government?*

They decided their first phase would focus on government agencies and public hiring practices. They didn't (yet) have the power to win on the national level. So they targeted local governments where they believed they had the ability to sway. *The campaign was finally ready to launch!*

Since its beginning in 2002, the "Ban the Box" campaign has successfully changed policies in over 100 cities and counties and over a dozen states.[46] Thousands upon thousands of potential public employees are no longer required to divulge their conviction history on job applications. In addition, the campaign has expanded to include pressuring some corporations, such as as Target, to follow suit. Years into the campaign, the struggle has gone national, with an ultimate goal of an executive order.[47]

The steps taken by All of Us or None to create and implement a campaign are only one example, but they suggest a general process that will be helpful for a variety of groups:

1. What issues move you or connect to your own story?
Campaigns can be long and drawn out. They take energy to maintain. It's great to pick a campaign centered on an issue that burns in your own heart from personal experience or a strong leaning.

2. Does your group share a strong, common thread?
The particular individuals who make up a group may have common concerns. A group of students may be attracted to certain campaigns that speak to them, for example, while a church group might be attracted to others. Groups might choose to use a process like "dotocracy" to identify shared values.

3. Listen to other people active in this issue.

Ask other seasoned organizers and directly impacted people. Find out what goals and campaigns excite them and interest them, and which they believe will significantly strengthen the movement.

4. Is there a local or national campaign you can join?

No need to build your own campaign if there's one you can join! If your group isn't driven to create a new campaign, then consider joining one that already exists. Looking at the above list or among allies, you may find a great fit in local or national campaigns led by people in prison or formerly incarcerated people to join (such as "ban the box" or fighting exorbitant costs of prison phone calls).

5. Spin the bottle.

I don't mean to sound crass, but some groups—especially groups who aren't directly impacted and want to "get it just right"—can waste years discussing what they *should* do. Much better to pick a small campaign, maybe one that might be completed in only a few months. That will create momentum, rather than waiting for the perfect opportunity to come along.

Whatever process your group uses to choose a campaign goal, don't forget some basic criteria to consider:
- The goal includes tangible benefits that impact people's lives;
- The goal is specific and may be achieved in an appropriate period of time;
- The people who will do the work feel motivated by the issue;
- The goal resonates with current and potential allies;
- The campaign has clear, identifiable targets—the people who can implement the needed change;
- The campaign helps connect the single-issue with other issues, movements, and seeing the bigger objectives of the movement.

REVOLUTIONARY REFORMS TO STORM THE CASTLE

As people think about goals, they often ask the question: *How can we make sure our movement addresses core, structural issues as opposed to merely making the current system a little more humane? How do we shift and transform public consciousness?*

There are no simple answers to these questions. If we had enough organized power to win our ultimate demands for change, it would be easy. But we don't. We don't have the power right now to make the massive changes needed to overturn the prison system, demilitarize and rebuild public schools, build a comprehensive health care system including support for mental health and addiction recovery services, provide affordable housing options to everyone, and rebuild our criminal justice system on the basis of reconciliation and restorative justice. But we have to start somewhere.

We can learn about this challenging aspect of campaigning from Mohandas Gandhi. Gandhi's aim for the Indian independence movement included kicking out the largest empire the world had ever seen. Yet one of his campaigns included a relatively minor goal. At the time, Britain held a monopoly on India's salt, keeping its production and distribution under strict control and taxing it heavily. In response, Gandhi led a 24-day, 240-mile march to the seashore, where he made salt in defiance of British law. That action kicked off a massive national civil disobedience campaign during which thousands of Indians made their own salt, all with a goal of forcing the British to surrender its unjust monopoly.

On the face of it, the campaign goal appeared relatively tame: *How could making salt kick out the British empire?* But Gandhi knew that the campaign would touch the Indian people. Everyone needed salt. Winning the campaign would build Indians' self-confidence and their sense of self-reliance, which the British empire had undermined for over a century by promoting dependency and a sense of helplessness. Gandhi sought goals that would build people's personal sense of power, their sense of control over their lives, their self-respect— and the people responded with a massive movement that ultimately broke British control of India.

This process of picking smaller campaigns that lead to bigger ones has been likened to storming a castle.[48] Castles are surrounded and protected by moats and military outposts. A system as complex and robust as mass incarceration has many, many moats and outposts protecting it. If our goal is to dismantle it, we have to start by crossing moats and removing outposts as we make our way toward the castle.

Such campaign goals might be called "outposts of reform." Winning them does not bring upheaval to the entire system. But it does build energy and strengthen our belief that we *can* make change. And, importantly, tackling outposts of reform gets us closer to the castle—especially when we help people see the issues so deeply that they join the quest for taking on the castle and not only the outpost right in front of them. The poetry committee at Tamms made that switch, moving from service to working for reforms, and ultimately fighting for the abolition of the prison itself.

Because they focus on smaller outposts of reform, campaigns tend to start at the local level, building up to bigger and bigger levels as the movement strengthens. This means that national organizations can hamper the efforts of local campaigns when they try to forcefully impose a strategy or ideological framework. Strong, healthy campaigns create spaces where people get to challenge each other on important movement questions: *Do we focus on the elimination of the worst prisons first, or target "average" prisons and expose how fundamentally wrong all of them are? Do we focus on slowing down the growth of prisons—for example, halting the massive expansion of detention centers for immigrants—or do we pour our efforts primarily into closing ones already in existence? Do we focus on prison abuse like solitary confinement or prison alternatives like restorative justice practices?*

Thinking about storming the castle helps keep us from merely looking at what is politically "realistic" and so only focusing narrowly on "achievable wins" in the immediate. Of course, some of our goals will seem politically unrealistic (if not, then we need bigger goals). Only by challenging the political realism of today are we going to transform it.

In that spirit, it's helpful to remember that not all campaigns are successful. But even unsuccessful campaigns can be immensely valuable. A good reminder about this comes from a near breaking point during the Montgomery bus boycott.

Because of high participation in the boycott, organizers needed to find rides for upwards of 30,000 to 40,000 bus boycotters. It was a massive logistical operation held together largely through the determination of a core group of women. To complicate matters, Montgomery city leaders dusted off a law against "private taxis" such as those used during the boycott—threatening to destroy the entire movement.

To solve the dilemma, Dr. King sought advice from T. J. Jemison, a leader in the ultimately unsuccessful Baton Rouge, Louisiana bus boycott of 1953. That boycott lasted only two weeks. But in the process, Jemison had faced this problem and found a way to skirt the law. They did this by running a citywide car pool in which people would "donate" to the movement organization per ride, which in turn would "donate" money to car owners and drivers.

This is a powerful reminder of the importance of campaigns learning from each other—and of recognizing that we stand on the shoulders of past campaigns, even if they weren't successful. The campaign that you run might be the Montgomery bus boycott, filled with historical glamor and garnering national and even international attention. Or your campaign might be the ill-fated 1953 bus boycott in Baton Rouge. But if other campaigns can learn lessons from your successes and failures, and if you can spawn leaders who carry on the struggle, then it wasn't in vain. We don't get a Montgomery success without the "failures" of past campaigns.

The struggle in Montgomery highlights another important strategic principle: don't shy away from boldness in your campaign—or escalating if your apparently tame goal doesn't work out. In Montgomery the original goals were very minor: respect on the buses, hiring black drivers for black routes, and a fixed dividing line between the black and white sections on the buses. There was nothing about the end of segregation.

It wasn't until virulent opposition made the chances of such modest goals seem bleak that the movement decided to escalate. In a stroke of both desperation and strategic insight, they expanded their demands to include full integration on the buses. *If they couldn't get their compromise, they might as well fight for what they really wanted.*

This kind of shift requires boldness. It takes courage for a group to move from minor objectives—like holding a public event or a book club—to objectives embedded with the possibility of head-on confrontation with authority. We can be reminded of the great abolitionist Frederick Douglass's words, "Power concedes nothing without a demand. It never did and it never will. Find out just what any people will quietly submit to and you have found out the exact measure of injustice and wrong which will be imposed upon them, and these will continue till they are resisted."

Once a group has selected an outpost of reform, it is ready to turn its attention to running an actual campaign. We of course hope the campaign wins. But whether a "success" or "failure," if the campaign helps people raise their eyes toward "the castle" and gets people ready to storm it, the group and its campaign have made a valuable contribution to the struggle.

USE THE SPECTRUM OF ALLIES

The spectrum of allies is a tool that helps us build better strategy by illustrating how and why campaigns succeed.[49] It's based on the assumption that "the public" is not a unified whole and that thinking about actions reaching "the public" is too fuzzy. And fuzzy intentions produce fuzzy results. Instead, it's helpful to sharply define our audience.

The spectrum of allies assumes that some people are in complete agreement and engaged with us (*active allies*), and others are completely opposed to our goals (*active opposition*). However, most people are somewhere in between those extremes. They might be *passive allies* or *passive opponents*—folks who might agree or disagree with you but aren't doing anything about it. Or they may be *neutrals*—genuinely undecided, completely uninformed, or truly apathetic.

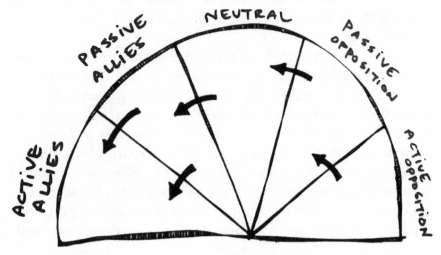

The tool brings with it some good news. Campaigns don't succeed by getting everyone to agree with us! In fact, in most successful campaigns, the *active opposition* don't change their minds (despite our best efforts). Rather, support for their position is pulled away by shifting the *passives* and *neutrals* one step in our direction (for example, moving *neutrals* to *passive allies*). What a relief!

With *passive allies* our goal is to engage them, finding small but concrete things that can bring them closer into the campaign so they can become engaged *active allies*: signing a petition (so you have their contact information), showing up to a march (but probably not a meeting, unless yours are unusually exciting), or bringing cupcakes to the next educational event (giving people tasks helps build their commitment). Passive allies are often looking for some way to connect to the issue and make a contribution. We have to design actions and events to engage them.

To move *neutrals,* we may expose them to people's lived experience in the face of injustice. If we can reach them, educational campaigns often stimulate *neutrals.* We want them to start feeling and thinking about the issue, and witnessing people discussing and taking a stand on it—so they can begin to develop their own stand on the issue as *passive allies.*

Neutrals are often moved by dramatic, emotional actions and images. We can draw from the example of Emmett Till, who was monstrously murdered by whites in 1955. His family held an open casket funeral where thousands lined up to mourn and bear witness to his butchered body. A photo of his face appeared in *Jet* magazine. Such actions could be replicated—imagine national open casket funerals in high-profile slayings by police to bring the violence into the open. This supports mourning, connects emotionally, and could help rehumanize "prisoners" to mainstream America.

With *passive opponents* we want to shift them away from their opposition and turn them into, at the very least, *neutrals.* In addition to touching their hearts with personal stories, it often helps to be deeply empathetic toward their views, while complicating their assumptions. Getting into their mindset can help to tease out complexities and hidden assumptions that they are not otherwise conscious of.

Groups often waste a huge amount of time obsessing over the *active opposition*, even though they rarely move. Efforts to move them, however, sometimes move other folks on the spectrum as they observe our clear-headed conviction and good intentions in the face of unyielding opposition.

The spectrum of allies tool can be used in meetings to assess where people and groups are on an issue. Healthy debates can emerge during this process, and it can expose our need for research, for example, *"Where does that union local stand on this issue?"* Debates may emerge about who to reach out to in order to help persuade other groups.

When using this tool, it's important to remind people to be specific. Instead of naming broad groups like "labor" or "children support groups," it's best to name specific groups or organizations, like "SEIU Local 1021" or "Children's Defense Fund." That's because the spectrum of allies is an *organizing* tool—it's useful in identifying who you are going to reach. That means the groups and individuals should be listed with names who can be contacted so you can reach out and engage with them.

The good news mentioned before is worth repeating. We don't need to convince everyone to become active allies to achieve our goals. Take the abolitionist movement against slavery in this country, as an example. If you add up every petition signed, every meeting, every public action—not even 1% of the population were *active allies*. Yet the movement was successful.

We therefore don't have to become distraught or immobilized trying to convince *active opponents*. Our work is to steadily move *passive allies, neutrals,* and *passive opponents* in our direction—while of course keeping our *active allies* engaged, too! As we rack up successes, campaigns begin to add up to a powerful social movement. And if we do it right, that movement can transform the whole society.

PROMOTE ALTERNATIVE INSTITUTIONS

Campaigns also offer a chance to promote alternative institutions. We would be naive to believe that private prison companies are not drawing up plans for alternatives if the prison system were to be radically challenged. Our work must also cultivate alternative structures as well.

Movements can build alternative institutions as part of their organizing. Think about the Black Panthers' breakfast program (later mimicked by the Head Start program). The Black Panthers started it as part of a movement program, to connect with people and to meet real, tangible needs.

Within the mass incarceration movement, alternative institutions include the work on restorative justice models that are being used in place of the traditional system. Immigrant communities are creating co-ops that stabilize people's income in the face of repression and deportation raids, while boosting movement participation. People are experimenting with other far-reaching institutions, including alternative schooling, alternative (non-lethal, non-retributive) policing methods, full employment policies, medical and mental care for all, and so on.

Youth Undoing Institutional Racism, for example, incorporates Freedom Schools into its organizing approach. At the Tyree Scott Freedom School, people learn about the history of racism, about the prison industrial complex, and about how different issues connect to each other.[50]

In Asheville, North Carolina, Immigration and Customs Enforcement (ICE) raided a parachute plant to sweep up all the undocumented immigrants working there. This is a common practice that is sometimes done by corporations to avoid paying their workers, or as political revenge against workers trying to organize. It is always destructive to the community. In this case, it was even more crass because both the city and the company knew about the ICE raid in advance—with a councilmember apparently inciting it with a phone call.

In this case, 57 people were detained. Because households that previously had two incomes lost one of their wage-earners, mostly husbands, the community spent tons of hours working on the ensuing economic problems.

Rather than just staying on the defensive and fighting legal cases, the community also developed their own home-cleaning cooperative. Nikki Marín Baena, one of the organizers, explains: "The business is exciting in itself: it does over $100,000 a year in sales—which is exciting for western NC—and the women make twice what they made before, as they build assets in the business. But the bigger point is the cooperative opened up an opportunity to make the women economically independent from their partners, allowing them to speak more critically about the relationships they were in, about the role of women in the immigrants rights movement, about domestic violence and strategies for economic independence of their community and others."[51]

Alternative institutions can be integrated and highlighted in our campaigns. For example, imagine if after a high-profile shooting by police of a black man, the family and community rejected the current legal process. "We don't want a grand jury investigation," they proclaim. "That determines if the government thinks something was legal or illegal. However, to stop the cycle, we have to hold ourselves to a higher standard. Clearly, harm was done here. More justice won't come from throwing someone in jail. We don't want our people going to prison—and we don't want the police going to prison either. Instead, we want a truly open restorative justice process to help heal the community." Following suit, the community could mobilize for an authentic restorative justice process, with the same vehemence as others who fight for legal retribution.

Again, effective campaigns are ones that promote and instill new values. To do that, we should look for all available opportunities to represent the highest moral values of humanity in our words and actions, and encourage others to do the same.

USE DILEMMA DEMONSTRATIONS

As campaigns develop, they often find that established channels—for example legal or lobbying—are insufficient. For that reason, groups often turn to various types of direct action, civil disobedience, or street protests. One way to strengthen that part of our campaigns is to create *dilemma demonstrations*.

Dilemma demonstrations are actions that force the target to either let you do what you want, or be shown as unreasonable as they stop you from doing it. For example, in a campaign I worked on against two giant unwanted casinos, the community was locked out at every step. No public input. No engagement. We were expected to roll over and give up.

We wanted more than a rally. We wanted a way to embed our movement's values in our action. So we set up a dilemma, giving a one-month notice that we wanted the release of all the previously secret documents concerning site plans, social impact studies, environmental plans, architectural renderings, and economic studies. "We are asking for all these documents to be made public by December 1 at high noon," we announced. "If they are not, then we will be forced to get them ourselves, going to the Gaming Control Board headquarters and performing a citizen's document search to liberate them and release them ourselves."

Our action was our message. And it placed those opposed to us in a tough dilemma. If they kept the documents secret, they confirmed public suspicions that they were hiding something nefarious. If they released the documents, we achieved a win for transparency. Either way, the movement won.

Dilemma demonstrations are different from rallies, marches, and vigils, which are all symbolic in nature. Dilemma demonstrations are effective because rather than *telling* about a problem, they *show* it. You can think of them as us taking a piece of our vision and implementing it now, with or without permission. That fills our demonstrations with action logic—helping the outsider understand the meaning of the action because its message is embedded in the action itself, not in a sign.

Dilemma demonstrations have been used to great effect:

- When refused service at lunch counters, black citizens kept sitting at the counter demanding to be served. They further highlighted the injustice by modeling dignified behavior;
- When national governments were secretly negotiating a massive "free trade" agreement that would undermine workers' and environmental rights (called the Free Trade Area of the Americas), a rag-tag group of protestors openly and publicly announced their intention to "liberate" the texts of the agreement through a "nonviolent search and seizure," which eventually led to the collapse of the talks;[52]
- Defying the law, some immigrant rights groups have openly offered "sanctuary" to folks facing final deportation orders. For example, New Sanctuary Movement of Philadelphia (NSM) provid-

ed sanctuary for mother-of-two Angela Navarro. She stayed in a church round-the-clock, during which she and others in NSM mobilized public pressure. Two months later she won a stay of deportation;[53]

- During the grueling sanctions against the people of Iraq by the US government, a group of peace activists with Voices in the Wilderness delivered basic medical aid to Iraqi civilians, in direct violation of the law—but in good conscience following their moral duty to help those suffering.

A grassroots group, Decarcerate PA, has experimented very creatively in creating stronger tactics in the direction of dilemma demonstrations. As part of their high-profile campaign to stop a $400 million two-prison complex, the group laid claim to the "first-ever act of civil disobedience to block prison construction in Pennsylvania." But they did it in a unique way: with seven people blocking the construction site by sitting at school desks complete with apples and notebooks. The logic speaks for itself: to pay for prisons, we are destroying our schools.[54]

Actions like this become even stronger as we reduce their symbolic nature. For example, imagine organizing a group of teachers and/or students going to the construction site to openly, transparently, and in all sincerity reclaim school supplies, like toilet paper or writing instruments, for their under-resourced schools. Or have students from overcrowded schools head to the site to hold class—"We'd have the money for more rooms if we weren't investing in prison expansion." Even if they weren't allowed onto the site, it would make a great civics class, great TV, and another chance to highlight how investing in prisons comes at the expense of schools.

By bringing dilemma demonstrations into our actions, we help others see the injustices in our present situation more acutely and with deeper emotion.

CONCLUSION

Using these tools and concepts we can wage important, meaningful campaigns. And yet, ultimately, it's not enough to win campaigns. Even lots of them. The yardstick of a movement is not how many campaigns are won, but how many hearts are moved and minds convinced to a new way of thinking and being.

Our movement must assess whether we are continually moving and recruiting people outside of our circles, growing the number of passive and active allies who will help play all sorts of roles in the movement. That means not just convincing people on a single issue, but on the breadth and depth of the problems in our current incarceration system and of the existence of viable, humane alternatives. We need broader agreement that we not only need to remove outposts of reform—we need to take down the castle.

Even as we engage others in one-on-one and group relationship building, we need to constantly re-examine ourselves, too. We need to clear out the smog inside of us, engaging in constant reflection about our own role in upholding the system of mass incarceration, in thought, word, and deed.

This all leads us back to finding our own power, and gearing up for powerful actions like Susan Burton's proposal to "crash the system." Our movement must keep getting bolder, recognizing that the entire system depends on our cooperation. If we can identify and take the risks necessary to remove that system's pillars of support, we can bring about fundamental change.

This is not easy. It requires us to connect with our humanity and our love, taking risks and facing down a monstrous system that's both external and inside of us. It requires that we build a new public consensus that values each and every human being's worth and dignity—especially poor people and people of color who are demonized, whether as felons, criminals, or any kind of "other."

If we don't do this deep work, new systems of racial and social control will continue to be born, even if mass incarceration adapts or fades away. But if we do this work, we can shape a new values system with love at its center that refuses to throw away any human life.

This is our call. This is our challenge.

We carry the encouragement from Dr. Martin Luther King Jr., "We must come to see that human progress never rolls in on the wheels of inevitability. It comes through the tireless efforts and the persistent work of dedicated individuals."[55]

May we each play our role in that tireless and persistent effort.

NEXT STEPS

1. Think about different campaign goals that might be a good match for your group. Read the chapter again for examples of goals and see what grabs you. What do you care about? What moves you? Pick a possible campaign goal.

2. Next, think about who has the ability to make the change you have chosen. That person or group is called the target. Spend some time researching your target: Who are they and what do they care about? What are their career ambitions? Who are they accountable to?

3. Spend time creating a list of five or more tactics that could put pressure on your target and help you achieve your goal. Organize them into a timeline that makes sense to you. It might be helpful to notice which tactics help your group step out of its current social circle. How can you use your tactics to reach new constituencies?

4. Are there ways you can incorporate alternative institutions into the timeline? What are ways you can talk about alternatives in your actions? Can some of those be inspiration for creating powerful dilemma demonstrations? Add any dilemma demonstrations into your timeline.

5. You now have a rough campaign draft. Share that campaign draft with others in your group and get their feedback.

6. Consider using the spectrum of allies at your group's next meeting or as part of a public event. It's valuable for groups interested in campaigning, and even those in the middle of campaigns, to assess who else they need to reach out to.

7. Think about the bigger issues raised in the conclusion. As you engage in your work, how do you also answer the broader challenges to build a movement not just of campaigns but changing fundamental social values? How is your group rising to that challenge? How could your group wrestle with that even more?

Get instructions on leading the spectrum of allies activity at: www.NewJimCrowOrganizing.org.

NOTES

Find additional resources, tools, handouts, and materials at: www.NewJimCrowOrganizing.org.

---

[1] Quoted by Gene Sharp in "The Technique of NVA," in *The Strategy of Civilian Defence*, ed. Adam Roberts (London: Faber and Faber, 1967), 97.

[2] James Ridgeway and Jean Casella, "America's 10 Worst Prisons: Pelican Bay," *Mother Jones*, May 8, 2013, www.motherjones.com/politics/2013/05/10-worst-prisons-america-pelican-bay.

[3] The first edition of this book called the first strike "tiny." Todd Ashker objected to that characterization, saying, "Our initial action was far from 'tiny'… it drew global attention, thanks to the great network of activists we were plugged into—who in turn had global connections, helping to ensure our action went global fast via net. It was also a much needed catalyst for breathing renewed life into the prisoner rights activist movement on the streets." This is another example of how history (and even well-meaning writers) minimize the power and growth of movements.

[4] Benjamin Wallace-Wells, "The Plot From Solitary," *New York* magazine, February 26, 2014, www.nymag.com/news/features/solitary-secure-housing-units-2014-2/.

[5] Bill Moyer, *Doing Democracy: The MAP Model for Organizing Social Movements* (Gabriola Island, BC, Canada: New Society Publishers, 2001).

[6] Get more information about ACJP's work, including their groundbreaking participatory defense (a community organizing model that dramatically brings activism into the court system), at www.acjusticeproject.org or 701 Lenzen Avenue, San Jose, CA 95126.

[7] Gail Noble, "Standing Up to the Court: How a mother and son called out the discrimination by a judge and the failures of an attorney," ACJP, accessed January 16, 2015, www.acjusticeproject.org/keycases/standing-up-to-a-racist-court/.

[8] Find out more about the Southern Coalition for Social Justice at www.southerncoalition.org or 1415 West Highway 54, Suite 101, Durham, NC 27707.

[9] Personal conversation with Daryl Atkinson.

[10] Angela Davis, *Are Prisons Obsolete?* (New York: Seven Stories Press, Open Media Series, 2003), 82.

[11] Jerry Elster, "After Twenty-Six Years in Prison: Reflections on Healing," *Tikkun*, January 3, 2012, www.tikkun.org/nextgen/after-twenty-six-years-in-prison-reflections-on-healing.

[12] To learn more about restorative justice, read Howard Zehr, *Changing Lenses: A New Focus for Crime and Justice* (Harrisonburg, VA: Herald Press, 2005), or visit Prison Fellowship International at www.restorativejustice.org or PO Box 17434, Washington, DC 20041 USA.

[13] Personal conversation with Jerry Elster, who can be contacted through AFSC (AFSC.org or 1501 Cherry Street, Philadelphia, PA, 19102) or All of Us or None (www.prisonerswithchildren.org/our-projects/allofus-or-none or 1540 Market St. Suite 490, San Francisco, CA 94102).

[14] Read more about the four roles of social change in Bill Moyer's book (cited above) or from the activist training organization Training for Change (www.TrainingForChange.org).

[15] More about Tina Reynolds' work is on WORTH's website (www.womenontherise-worth.org or 171 E. 122nd St. Suite 2R, New York, NY 10035). She is also co-editor of *Interrupted Life: Experiences of Incarcerated Women in the United States* (Oakland, CA: University of California Press, 2010).

[16] Bureau of Justice Statistics, "Women Offenders" (Washington, DC: US Department of Justice, 1999), 8.

[17] Victoria Law and Tina Reynolds, "Birthing Behind Bars: Fighting for Reproductive Justice for Women in Prison," *AlterNet*, May 10, 2012,

www.alternet.org/story/155378/birthing_behind_bars%3A_fighting_for_repro ductive_justice_for_women_in_prison.

[18] For example, see Berit Lakey and George Lakey, *Grassroots and Nonprofit Leadership* (Gabriola Island, BC, Canada: New Society Publishers, 1998) and Kimberley A. Bobo et al., *Organizing for Social Change: Midwest Academy Manual for Activists* (Newport Beach, CA: Seven Locks Press, 2001).

[19] Marc Lamont Hill, "Why Aren't We Fighting for CeCe McDonald?" *Ebony*, June 11, 2012, www.ebony.com/news-views/why-arent-we-fighting-for-cece-mcdonald.

[20] Parker Marie Molloy, "WATCH: CeCe McDonald Makes First Television Appearance Following Release from Men's Prison," the *Advocate*, January 21, 2014, www.advocate.com/politics/transgender/2014/01/21/watch-cece-mcdonald-makes-first-television-appearance-following.

[21] For more on Rosa Parks's early activism, read Danielle L. McGuire, *At the Dark End of the Street: Black Women, Rape, and Resistance—A New History of the Civil Rights Movement from Rosa Parks to the Rise of Black Power* (New York: Vintage, 2011).

[22] Adapted slightly from Si Kahn, *Creative Community Organizing: A Guide for Rabble-Rousers, Activists, and Quiet Lovers of Justice* (Oakland, CA: Berrett-Koehler Publishers, 2010), 171-172.

[23] The number of immigrant detainees was up to 429,247 in 2011, more than doubled from a few years prior. See National Immigration Forum, *The Math of Immigration Detention: Runaway Costs for Immigration Detention Do Not Add Up to Sensible Policies* (Washington, DC: National Immigration Forum, 2012).

[24] Personal conversation with Gail Tyree, who now sits on the board of Grassroots Leadership, which can be reached at www.grassrootsleadership.org or (704) 332-3090 or 2121 Commonwealth Ave, Suite 105, Charlotte, NC 28205.

[25] "Why the Climate Movement Must Stand with Ferguson," 350.org, www.350.org/how-racial-justice-is-integral-to-confronting-climate-crisis/.

[26] Srdja Popovic et al., *Nonviolent Struggle: 50 Crucial Points* (Belgrade, Serbia: CANVAS, 2006), www.usip.org/sites/default/files/nonviolent_eng.pdf. The training group CANVAS was founded by leaders in Otpor.

[27] A well-produced movie about Otpor and nonviolent movement-building is *Bringing Down a Dictator,* directed by Steve York (Washington, DC: A Force More Powerful Films, 2001), DVD.

[28] Richard K. Taylor, *Blockade!: A Guide to Non-Violent Intervention* (Maryknoll, NY: Orbis Books, 1977).

[29] Susan Burton's proposal is mentioned in a March 10, 2012, *New York Times* op-ed by Michelle Alexander, "Go to Trial: Crash the Justice System," www.nytimes.com/2012/03/11/opinion/sunday/go-to-trial-crash-the-justice-system.html. You can read about Susan Burton's work with A New Way of Life at www.anewwayoflife.org or 323-563-3575 or 11211 SW Avenue, Los Angeles, CA 90059.

[30] Mia Murrietta, "Justice for Trayvon Martin: Why Punishing His Killer Isn't Enough," *Ella's Voice*, July 17, 2013, www.ellabakercenter.org/blog/2013/07/justice-for-trayvon-martin-why-punishing-his-killer-isnt-enough.

[31] Examples of groups going beyond calls for retributive justice include "Indicting a System Not a Man....," *Prison Culture*, November 16, 2014, www.usprisonculture.com/blog/2014/11/16/indicting-a-system-not-a-man and Fania Davis, "This Country Needs a Truth and Reconciliation Process on Violence Against African Americans—Right Now," *Yes! Magazine*, December 3, 2014, www.yesmagazine.org/peace-justice/this-country-needs-a-truth-and-reconciliation-process-on-violence-against-african-americans

[32] Eddie Ellis, "An Open Letter to Our Friends on the Question of Language," Center for NuLeadership on Urban Solutions, 2007, www.centerfornuleadership.org/current-projects/the-languge-letter-campaign/.

[33] Some training opportunities to work on anti-oppression come from Training for Change (www.trainingforchange.org), The Catalyst Project (www.collectiveliberation.org), and the Racial Equity Institute (rei.racialequityinstitute.org).

[34] Berit Lakey and George Lakey, *Grassroots and Nonprofit Leadership* (Gabriola Island, BC, Canada: New Society Publishers, 1998), 28.

[35] Lakey, page 31.

[36] From the radio documentary, "The Formerly Incarcerated and Convicted People's Movement: The Struggle for Freedom and Transformation Continues," from the series "Bringing Down the New Jim Crow," produced by Chris Moore-Backman, www.prx.org/series/32471. Reverend Glasgow founded The Ordinary People Society, featured in Shaila Dewan, "In Alabama, a Fight to Regain Voting Rights Some Felons Never Lost," *New York Times*, March 2, 2008, www.nytimes.com/2008/03/02/us/02felons.html.

[37] "History of the FICPM," ficpmovement.wordpress.com/about/history-of-the-ficpm/.

[38] See Nazgol Ghandnoosh, PhD, *Race and Punishment: Racial Perceptions of Crime and Support for Punitive Policies* (Washington, DC: The Sentencing Project, 2014), www.atlanticphilanthropies.org/sites/default/files/uploads/Report-Race-and-Punishment.pdf.

[39] Maya Schenwar, *Locked Down, Locked Out: Why Prison Doesn't Work and How We Can Do Better* (Oakland, CA: Berrett-Koehler Publishers, 2014).

[40] This is obviously not even close to a comprehensive list. One resource for creating campaigns is Nation Inside (www.nationinside.org), which helps groups create "campaign hubs" to help recruit people, gather stories, and build a database of activists.

[41] See, for example, Jeff Deeney, "A Philadelphia School's Big Bet on Nonviolence," *The Atlantic*, July 18, 2013, www.theatlantic.com/national/archive/2013/07/a-philadelphia-schools-big-bet-on-nonviolence/277893/. To learn more about Alternatives to Violence Project, see www.avpusa.org or 1050 Selby Ave., St. Paul MN 55104.

[42] Paul Tullis, "Can Forgiveness Play a Role in Criminal Justice?" *New York Times*, January 4, 2013, www.nytimes.com/2013/01/06/magazine/can-forgiveness-play-a-role-in-criminal-justice.html.

[43] From the video "Enough is Enough," All of Us or None, www.youtube.com/watch?v=Sw56f6Vbqhs#t=381. See other videos: www.prisonerswithchildren.org/our-projects/allofus-or-none/all-of-us-or-none-videos.

[44] Alicia Bannon, Mitali Nagrecha and Rebekah Diller, "Criminal Justice Debt: A Barrier to Reentry," Brennan Center for Justice, 2010, www.brennancenter.org/sites/default/files/legacy/Fees%20and%20Fines%20FINAL.pdf.

[45] Michael Collins, "When Police 'Reforms' Only Legitimize Police Abuses," *In These Times*, December 9, 2014, www.inthesetimes.com/article/17427/when_police_reforms_only_legitimize_police_abuses. Also read another critique in this vein: "Police 'Reforms' You Should Always Oppose..." *Prison Culture*, December 1, 2014, www.usprisonculture.com/blog/2014/12/01/police-reforms-you-should-always-oppose.

[46] An updated list of municipalities with bans is available from the National Employment Law Project, www.nelp.org/page/-/SCLP/Ban-the-Box-Fair-Chance-State-and-Local-Guide.pdf.

[47] Dorsey Nunn, "It's Time for an Executive Order to Ban the Box," TalkPoverty.org, October 10, 2014, www.talkpoverty.org/2014/10/10/executive-order-ban-the-box/.

[48] Martin Oppenheimer and George Lakey, *A Manual for Direct Action* (Chicago: Quadrangle Books, 1965).

[49] Read more about the spectrum of allies and other strategy tools on Training for Change's website, www.trainingforchange.org.

[50] Learn more at www.afsc.org/category/topic/tyree-scott-freedom-school or contact them at 1501 Cherry St, Philadelphia, PA 19102.

[51] Personal conversation with Nikki Marín Baena.

[52] Philippe Duhamel, "The Dilemma Demonstration: Using nonviolent civil disobedience to put the government between a rock and a hard place," New Tactics in Human Rights, 2004, www.newtactics.org/resource/dilemma-demonstration-using-nonviolent-civil-disobedience-put-government-between-rock-and.

[53] New Sanctuary Movement, "Angela's Story," www.sanctuaryphiladelphia.org/index.php/campaigns/sanctuary-for-families/angela-s-story.

[54] "November 19 Action and Tribunal roundup," *Decarcerate PA*, November 2012, www.decarceratepa.info/content/protest.

[55] Martin Luther King Jr., "Remaining Awake Through a Great Revolution," speech at the National Cathedral, Washington, DC, March 31, 1968 (Congressional Record, 9 April 1968, mlk-kpp01.stanford.edu/index.php/kingpapers/article/remaining_awake_through_a_great_revolution/).

9 780988 550810